The POWER of MARK'S STORY

The POWER of MARK'S STORY

Mitzi L. Minor

CHALICE
PRESS

ST. LOUIS, MISSOURI

Cover art: "Look at the Birds of the Air," by Tadao Tanaka
Cover and interior design: Elizabeth Wright
Art direction: Elizabeth Wright

This book is printed on acid-free, recycled paper.

Visit Chalice Press on the World Wide Web at
www.chalicepress.com

10 9 8 7 6 5 4 3 2 1   01 02 03

Library of Congress Cataloging-in-Publication Data

Minor, Mitzi, 1958–
    The power of Mark's story / Mitzi L. Minor.
        p.   cm.
    Includes bibliographical references and index.
    ISBN 0-8272-2974-7 (alk. paper)
    1. Bible. N. T. Mark–Criticism, Narrative. I. Title.
    BS2585.52 .M56   2002
    226.3 ' 066–dc21   2001004596

Printed in the United States of America

Contents

For

Dianne, Mary Lin, and Jenny,

companions on the journey,

keepers of the stories,

friends

Preface

A few years ago during a family vacation to the beach, after the little children had been put to bed, my mother, my two sisters, and I gathered in one of the bedrooms of our rented condo. My oldest niece, who was about eleven at the time, joined us. For a couple of hours we told stories of the crazy things my sisters and I had done when we were teenagers (including a few things I think my mom hadn't known about till that night). We laughed until our sides ached and the tears flowed. Finally we decided enough was enough, and it was time for bed. But my niece begged us, "No, don't stop. Tell some more stories."

I know how she felt. I cannot remember a time in my life when I was not surrounded by stories or when I didn't love them. My parents read story books to me from the time I was very small. I especially loved Dr. Seuss' *Horton Hears a Who*, but I also vividly remember fairy tales and Bible stories (I was captivated by Joseph's whole saga). Riding in the car with my dad gave me chances to hear his stories of growing up during World War II in a small town in Alabama. Sometimes I'd sit in the back bedroom while my mom ironed and hear stories of her family and what life was like when I was a baby. In elementary school I discovered *My Friend Flicka*, the Hardy Boys, and *The Witch of Blackbird Pond*. Later Herman Wouk's *The Winds of War* and *War and Remembrance* first made the Holocaust real to me. Harper Lee's *To Kill a Mockingbird* and Will Campbell's *Brother to a Dragonfly* did the same for me regarding race issues. My college tennis teammates teased me about J. R. R. Tolkien being a constant companion. At some point I found the wealth of wisdom in Jewish folk tales. In my adulthood I have been profoundly marked by the novels of Chaim Potok and Alice Walker. When my nieces and nephews came along, I "returned the favor" and gladly read stories to them, rediscovering Winnie the Pooh (and Tigger too) in the process. I have also told them some of the family stories I learned from my parents. And always there were those Bible stories.

Imagine, then, how thrilled I was to sit in Dr. Edward Thornton's class on The Psychology of the Religious Experience and listen to him talk about the power of stories. Here I was, a graduate student in a graduate class in the fall of 1984, hearing a respected professor talk quite seriously about stories and their impact in our lives! I had sensed for so long that stories were far more than entertainment for us. Now Dr. Thornton was saying out loud in an academic setting that something I had intuited was indeed true! The experience was profoundly affirming. In addition, he taught me the words to express the power of stories in our lives and gave me the means to explore how and why stories are so powerful. In many ways I have never "recovered" from studying with Dr. Thornton. I hope I never do. My gratitude to him and for him is boundless.

One final comment about that class: at some point during the semester I thought to myself, "I wonder why we never read biblical stories like Dr. Thornton is teaching us to read journey stories." That thought lodged itself in the back of my brain and never left. It sat there and waited all during the years as I studied and became a professor of New Testament. Then, when the faculty of the Central Baptist Theological Seminary in Kansas City invited me to give their 1999 New Testament Lectures, that thought saw its chance. It pushed itself to the surface of my conscious thinking and became the basis for the lectures I gave there. I am grateful to the people of CBTS for giving me an "excuse" to explore a thought I had wondered about many years previously. I am especially thankful to CBTS faculty members Molly Marshall and David May, longtime teachers and friends, who were instrumental in my being invited to lecture at their seminary.

Further work on "that thought" resulted in the 2000 Bowen Lectures that I gave at my own seminary, Memphis Theological Seminary. I owe special thanks to my colleagues on the faculty at MTS for their interest, support, and encouragement of my work. I am so lucky–every day I get to practice my vocation among some of the most genuine people on earth. I am also grateful to students in my classes on Mark, especially the class that met during the fall of 2000 as I was finishing this book. Their enthusiasm for Mark's story and for the work I was pursuing, and their insightfulness spurred me on. Before leaving the subject of MTS, thanks are also due the library staff for their help in my research. My good friend Nancy McSpadden, in her role as acquisitions librarian, kept an especially watchful eye for new books that might help me–thanks, Nance.

My editor at Chalice Press, Jon L. Berquist, worked with me for two years as "that thought" struggled to become a book. For all the time given to "bouncing ideas around," for the editorial advice, and for the friendship Jon gave me I am grateful. For being the kind of editor who affirmed me for taking his suggestions "seriously but not automatically," I am particularly grateful.

My parents, Georgia and Larry Minor, have been like Horton in *Horton Hears a Who* for me. I have never doubted that they would look until they found me, even on the "three millionth flower," should I ever get lost. I am so thankful for that. And for the Bible stories they read to me when I was a child. To them, to Dee Cooke and Jill Brown (my sisters), to Mitchell Cooke and Jeff Brown (my brothers-in-law), to Ashley, Tyler, Courtney, Ryan, Carter, and Devin (my nieces and nephews), I wish to say thanks for the love and laughter and for sharing my stories. I also want to say to my nieces and nephews: you need to read stories more!

Finally, I wish to acknowledge three special people whom I am lucky enough to call friends. The world is a more hopeful place because Dianne Oliver, Mary Lin Hudson, and Jenny Stone are in it. My life is much richer because they love me and let me love them. And my work is immeasurably better because of their help and insightfulness. Each of them has heard and read significant portions of this material and critiqued it. They have been my conversation partners throughout the months of trying to get "that thought" to become a book. When the process threatened to overwhelm me, they were encouragement itself. Their very presence in my life pushes me to grow as a human being, which can only make my work better. Because they value me as a child of God, I am better able to do so as well, but I can absolutely bear witness that they never let me take myself too seriously! And so, I dedicate this book to them with deep, deep gratitude.

I am finishing this book during the season of Advent. In a variety of times and places in these weeks we will tell and re-tell a story about shepherds and angels, a poor peasant girl becoming a mother, and a baby wrapped in swaddling clothes and lying in a manger. That story is not in Mark's gospel, but it is one of the *good* stories in my world. Completing this work in these days makes me smile.

Advent, 2000
Memphis, Tennessee

INTRODUCTION
The Power of a Story

A friend of mine who moved from Chicago to Mississippi about the time he entered college once told me that a major adjustment he had to make was to Southern storytelling. He was struck that when Southern people want to relate something important, they usually tell a story rather than offer an explanation. I was hardly knocked off my feet by his observation. After all, I grew up in the land of Mark Twain, Harper Lee, William Faulkner, Flannery O'Connor, Alice Walker, and even John Grisham today (among many others). Southerners have no monopoly on storytelling, of course. Indeed, note this story from the Ekoi people of Africa:

> Mouse goes everywhere. Through rich men's houses she creeps, and visits even the poorest. At night, with her little bright eyes, she watches the doing of secret things and no treasure chamber is so safe but she can tunnel through and see what is hidden there. In the old days she wove a story child from all that she saw, and to each of these she gave a gown of different colors—white, red, blue, and black. The stories became her children and lived in her house and served her, because she had no children of her own.

The story then takes a long and seemingly irrelevant turn as it tells of Leopard and Sheep trying to trick each other in a time of hunger. Leopard chases Sheep's daughter to a crossroads where they go separate ways. Then Sheep's daughter meets a Nimm woman whose "medicine" Sheep takes. The woman is angry, so she chases Sheep:

> In her hurry to escape, Sheep ran against the door of the house where Mouse lived. The door was old and it broke and the stories on earth and all the histories ran out. After that they never went back to dwell with Mouse any more, but remained running up and down all over the earth.[1]

1

So stories are "all over the earth." Poet Muriel Rukeyser even claims, "The Universe is made of stories, not atoms."[2] I cherish having grown up in a culture that taught me to be aware of and attentive to the power of stories.

As far as biblical scholars can hypothesize from available evidence, the writer of Mark's gospel was the first of the early Christians to present a sustained written account of Jesus of Nazareth.[3] Given my cultural heritage, I am not surprised that this writer chose to pen a story about Jesus rather than a theological treatise. I've read stories, and I've read theology books. Ask me which ones I've read twice! Thus, in this book, I am bringing together two of the loves of my life: the human art of storytelling and Mark's gospel as a story. I want to see what we may learn as people of faith if we apply the insights gained from storytelling to Mark's story.

Let me begin with descriptions of stories and the reasons we tell them. Students of storytelling note that people of all cultures, places, and times have told stories. As novelist Ursula K. Le Guin says, "There have been societies that did not use the wheel, but there have been no societies that did not tell stories."[4] Perhaps this human reality is primarily due to the narrative quality of human experience: The episodes of our lives take place one after another, as in a story. We even think in stories so that we can weave together into a coherent whole all the people, dates, and facts that fill our lives.[5] Theologian and storyteller John Shea calls human beings "natural narrative beings" who love to tell the stories of the experiences that are important to them.[6]

Some of the stories we tell entertain us. Others teach us moral lessons. Many of these stories are the ones we tell our children. For this reason some people consider stories to be unsophisticated fictions best left behind for the wordy reasoning and abstract ideas of adulthood. But such a perspective misses the reality that some stories are told and retold for generations because they touch a deep, spiritual place in our lives.[7] They are composed of inspired layers of underlying truth that invite us to hear, but do not force themselves on us. These stories help us understand our own stories. They remind us of who we are, and from whence we have come. They help us along our way to remember what it means to be authentically human.[8] In the words of theologian Dorothee Soelle, this means the stories call us to come home to ourselves, to live the unfragmented lives for which we long, free of fear and calculation and filled with trust, hope, and love as God intended.[9] They also relate our failures, lacks, and losses. Never underestimate the power of stories to unsettle us by making us face the ragged edges of life. Thus, theologian Sallie McFague has declared, "In a sense, any story is about ourselves, and a good story is *good* precisely because it somehow rings true to human life. We recognize our own pilgrimages from here to there in a good story; we feel its movement in our bones and know it is 'right'."[10]

As a person of faith, I am particularly interested in how many of these *good* stories may be called *sacred* stories. They heed the Presence of God that hides in every breath, in every word and sound and silence, waiting to be found out and brought home. Theologian C. S. Song likes stories because the world there is the world of real people of flesh and blood, not of abstract theological ideas and concepts. Such "real people" strive to reveal the divine light shining in the darkness of their hearts and in the depths of their community. And sometimes they succeed.[11]

When these *good* stories "shine their divine light in the darkness," they offer us a sense of resolution and truth. They sustain us with illumination and heal us.[12] Indeed, we might say that story is the language of faith. As storyteller Jerre Roberts points out, "all major religions communicate through story. We find their core belief, their wisdom, not in carefully formulated creeds and canons and laws, but in their foundational stories."[13] Soelle reminds us that the language of the Bible speaks of God most often in narrative rather than dogma.[14] Again, we should hardly be knocked off our feet by these observations. When we reflect a bit, we can sense how essential stories are if we wish to share with others our deepest spiritual insights and experiences. Along with other imaginative forms (i.e., poetry, art, music), stories are capable of bringing the whole of our experiences of God to light in ways that abstract intellectualizing is not.[15] How many of us have begun to relate a moving spiritual experience by saying, "It was like…" and then completed the sentence with a "narrative" of some kind ("it was like Jonah getting out of the belly of the whale," or "it was like the sun coming up in the morning")? Explain the experience? No, we cannot. But a story allows us to communicate it and thus to share it with others. Note Soelle's words again: "Whatever is living testimony of the life humans live today cannot be summed up in statistics and press releases. Prayer and narrative shun that form of communication; its inherent frigidity would kill them."[16]

So we can agree with writer Jane Yolen that there is no argument: Stories are powerful.[17] Perhaps we are ready to appreciate the following Jewish folktale:

> Whenever misfortune threatened the Jews, Rabbi Israel Baal Shem Tov would retreat to the forest, light the fire, say the prayer and the misfortune would be avoided. In the passing of time this task fell to a second rabbi who knew both the place in the forest and the prayer but not how to light the fire. Nevertheless, the misfortune was avoided. A third rabbi knew only the place; the prayer and the fire had been forgotten. But this too was enough and the misfortune was avoided. Finally the task fell to Rabbi Israel of Rizhyn who knew neither the place nor the fire nor the prayer. All he could do was tell the story. And it was sufficient.[18]

So we are reading along, and suddenly we find ourselves in a story. What happens to us? Perhaps we are encouraged by Little Toot's "I think I can, I think I can." To tell a personal "story," I have never forgotten the moment when, as a small child, my dad read to me Dr. Seuss's *Horton Hears a Who*. In the story Horton the elephant searches for the tiny Whos, who are lost in a clover patch a hundred miles wide. He searches "on through the afternoon, hour after hour… Till he found them at last! On the three millionth flower."[19] Still today I remember how warm and safe I felt as I sensed that there are "Hortons" (such as my parents) in the world who would not rest until they found me, should I be lost.

At other times we may well be stopped cold, startled by what we find, challenged to reevaluate our priorities and imagine a better self and world. We discover that we want to be like the child who cries, "The emperor has no clothes on!" But perhaps we have been more like those in the crowd who go along with the deceptions all around us. Once upon a time Winnie the Pooh and Piglet joined Rabbit in a plan to get Tigger lost in the woods and leave him there till the next morning. Then he would be a "Humble Tigger…a Sad Tigger, a Melancholy Tigger, a Small and Sorry Tigger and Oh-Rabbit-I-*am*-glad-to-see-you-Tigger" who would then not bounce so much when they asked him not to, because his bouncing was getting on Rabbit's nerves. Rabbit, however, was the one who got lost in the woods. In the end, Tigger, with his high and loud bouncing, found the "Very Small and Sorry" Rabbit.[20] The story may gently urge us to wonder if we are like Rabbit, wanting others to behave themselves as we think they should and live their lives as conveniently for us as possible. The truth presented by the story, however, is that we all benefit when all of us are allowed, even encouraged, to be exactly who we are. Or there is Opus the penguin in Berkeley Breathed's *A Wish for Wings That Work* who asked Santa one year for wings that would have him flying like other birds on Christmas morning. But on Christmas Eve the harness on Santa's sleigh broke. The sleigh, with Santa on board, landed in an icy cold lake and began to sink. The snow ducks awakened Opus, who used his nonflying penguin wings to swim swiftly to Santa and tow him to shore.[21] The story may surprise us into realizing that we too have spent so much time longing for what we haven't that we underdevelop and never share the gifts and abilities we already have.

So *good* stories indeed are powerful. They can save us by comforting and encouraging us when the struggle to be authentically human seems hopeless in this crazy world of ours. They also nudge us toward authenticity by narrating new possibilities for living and calling us to conversion when we are being less than we were created to be.

Do you sense, as I do, that it is no accident that Mark presents Jesus as a master storyteller? Or that Mark chose to write a *good* story about Jesus rather than a theological treatise?

Biblical scholars, however, have been little interested in Mark's gospel as a story. In particular, biblical scholars have not pursued ways Mark's story might sustain us with illumination and heal us. Or how it may act as a source of conversion and transformation for us by narrating how we may be authentically human, as God created us to be. Even narrative critics have been more interested in how the gospel writer worked his craft than with the impact of the story that actually was crafted. My intent in this book is to attend to this neglected aspect of Mark. I want to take advantage of Mark's having written a story about Jesus by reading the gospel through lenses suggested by those who love telling, hearing, and reading *good* stories.

Since stories are retold for generations because they touch a deep spiritual place in our lives and show us how to be authentically human, our reading lens means that the driving question in this book is, What might Mark's story show us about being human, as God created us to be? We will try to answer this question by reading Mark alongside other *good* stories. Something wonderful happens when we do so. For many of us, the biblical stories are so familiar that we have grown dull to the shock, delight, and enlightenment they offer. Or we've heard the stories interpreted in only one way so that we have become closed to new meanings and insights that could be there. So we've stopped having "Aha!" moments with the biblical texts. But other stories may not be so familiar. Placing them alongside Mark's stories can shed new light, help us see the stories differently, and gain fresh insights about being authentically human from them.[22]

In the last moment of this introduction, I wish to make two disclaimers, or perhaps I should call them confessions, about my efforts here. First, I recognize that some may protest that the church has declared Mark's gospel to be sacred literature that is inspired by the Spirit. It should not, therefore, be compared to other kinds of stories. I wish in no way to diminish our appreciation of Mark as sacred literature by relating it to other stories. Instead, since the Bible is, in C. S. Song's words, "a world of stories in the world of stories," I believe that the world of stories at large and the world of stories in the Bible can illumine each other and deepen our experience of God.[23]

Second, I confess that the "hunches" presented here about where inspired layers of truth might lie in *good* stories and in Mark's gospel are those of an educated, white, North American (in this sense, privileged), feminist, Christian woman minister (in this sense, often a victim of oppression). As is true for all Bible readers, who I am naturally shapes my hunches and how I respond to them. I present my hunches and ask readers to search and struggle through Mark's text with me. But I must warn us all: If we should indeed find truth there as we search, then we will have to decide if we have the courage to take it to heart.[24]

CHAPTER 1

THE BEGINNING OF THE STORY

"Prepare the Way of the Lord"
(Mark 1:3)

MIDWAY ON LIFE'S JOURNEY, I woke up and found myself in a dark wood, for I had lost my path…

As I was stumbling down, there suddenly appeared before my eyes a figure who seemed to be voiceless from long silence. When I saw him in this deserted place, I cried, "Have pity on me, whatever you are, ghost or living man!"

He answered me, "No man, though once a man…I was a poet, and praised the righteous son of Anchises, who sailed from Troy after it was destroyed by flames."…"You must journey on another road," he answered me when he saw my tears, "if you want to escape from this wilderness."

"You have convinced me to go with you just as I first intended. Now let's go on with one heart—you as the guide, leader, and teacher!"

As soon as I said it, he started moving on; and then I started down that steep and savage path."[1]

DANTE, *INFERNO*

"LOOK! I am sending my messenger before you who will prepare your way, a voice of one crying in the wilderness, 'Prepare the way of the Lord...'"

John the baptizer appeared in the wilderness...and he preached saying, "The one who is stronger than me is coming after me..."

It happened in those days that Jesus came from Nazareth of Galilee and was baptized in the Jordan by John. And immediately upon coming up from the water he saw the heavens being ripped open and the Spirit as a dove coming down into him. And a voice happened from heaven, "You are my son the beloved; in you I am well pleased."

And immediately the Spirit drove him into the wilderness. And he was in the wilderness forty days being tempted by Satan...

After John was betrayed, Jesus came into Galilee preaching the gospel of God and saying, "The time is fulfilled and the basileia of God has drawn near."

—————————————————————————— MARK 1:2–15

When Dante Alighieri penned his classic story in the early 1300s of a pilgrim's journey through hell (the inferno) and purgatory to paradise, he was drawing on a deep and wide tradition of using "journey" as a metaphor for life, especially the spiritual life. People of all cultures, times, and places have told journey stories about heroes and heroines on quests for paradise, the holy grail, the Celestial City, or some other elusive something that would give purpose to their lives. For every person who has told these stories, there are many others who have listened to or read them as they seek to understand their own living. Perhaps most folks do not consider themselves heroes. Nonetheless, they hope that paradise is "out there" somewhere and that in their living they might discover the way to get there.

Consequently, we will do well to note that Mark has shaded his story of Jesus with the colors of a journey story in ways that touch our own desire to understand our living. We can begin to understand some of what Mark has to teach us about being authentically human if we attend to these colors. The goal in this chapter is to do exactly that. First, we'll discuss journey stories generally to show their pervasiveness, their movements, and their significance and power. Second, we'll examine closely Mark's beginning to see how Mark invites us to read this story of Jesus as a journey story. Finally, we'll describe ways that reading Mark's story in this way can be significant for those of us committed to our own spiritual journeys so that we become more fully the human beings God created us to be.

The Ascent (Journey) to God

There is an old, old wisdom that sees all of life as a spiritual journey, including the possibility that someone's life consists of a spiritual journey not taken. Spiritually sensitive folk have always been drawn to the metaphor of "journey" to describe their growth toward communion with God. Christians are no exception. Gregory of Nyssa (ca. 335–ca. 395) may have been the first Christian mystic to describe the spiritual life as an "ascent to God," but he was not the last. Others, such as John of the Cross and Teresa of Avila (both in the sixteenth century) followed with descriptions of their experiences of the spiritual journey. Thus, today there is a widespread awareness of a classical mystical teaching regarding the purgative (letting go of worldly things), illuminative (transcending the self during the "dark night of the soul"), and unitive (communion with God) stages that one must pass through if one wishes to journey to God. Together these three stages are often called the "purgative way."[2]

Meanwhile, storytellers in all places and times have told tales of those who made pilgrimages to holy places. Because these were journeys not only of space but also of spirit, the traveler was transformed along the way. Then she or he returned to bring wisdom and healing to those back home. Ancient Egyptians recounted the journeys of Isis to find Osiris after Osiris had been captured and cast away by his evil brother Set. Isis wished to return Osiris to Egypt, for he was the author of creativity and life. Native Americans tell many such stories. Among these are Sayadio's search for his dead sister's spirit so that he could give her life again, and the story of "Jumping Mouse," who heard the roar of the river and got a glimpse of the Sacred Mountains, which he then traveled to find. Dante wrote his poem of the journey to Paradise from Italy in the early 1300s, while John Bunyan penned his tale of Christian's quest for the Celestial City (the classic story of *The Pilgrim's Progress*) from England in the 1670s. In their collection of fairy tales first published in Germany in 1812, the brothers Grimm included the story of a king's three sons who each made a journey to find "The Golden Bird." In the latter part of the twentieth century J. R. R. Tolkien wrote at length of Frodo's journey to the center of the Land of Mordor to destroy the Ring that would give Sauron, the evil lord, all power over Middle-earth (Tolkien's trilogy is entitled *The Lord of the Rings*).

Outwardly these stories, and all the many like them, are about certain characters having specific adventures as they pursue particular goals or destinations. Fundamentally, however, these stories are about inner journeys. They tell of persons seeking meaning for their lives. Every feeling or impulse, every turning point in a life, every spiritual experience or insight is depicted in the stories as an object or action. An interpreter can relate these objects and actions to experiences of the soul on its journey through life. Then the stories have a transforming effect on readers/hearers, for they offer guidance to those who have embarked on their own inner, spiritual journeys.[3]

The Stages of the Journey

The journeys the pilgrims undertake, whether presented in "the vast, almost oceanic images of the Orient, in the vigorous narratives of the Greeks, or in the majestic legends of the Bible,"[4] are made up of stages through which pilgrims must pass. First, there is a summons of some kind, a sense of "call." Dorothee Soelle says that prior to the summons, everything seems fine. But there comes a sense that something is lacking or lost or inexplicable. Then someone gets the idea of looking for or demanding something that is not "here."[5] She or he must go "there" to find it. The journey begins. Pilgrims soon must cross a "first threshold," that is, the first realization that the journey will not be easy. So this threshold becomes the first temptation to turn back. Those who continue receive spiritual aid, travel the road of trials, and pass through the belly of the whale or the dark night of the soul–choose your favorite metaphor for the most gut-wrenching moments on the way–during which pilgrims may despair of their very lives. When they find themselves not dead but alive (even reborn) and having attained the goal of their quest, they return home to renew their people.[6]

The Lure of Journey Stories

Why are journey stories so pervasive? Answering such "why" questions definitively is notoriously difficult, but we can guess some reasons these stories are common. One possibility is that many of us think of our lives, consciously or unconsciously, as a journey. Perhaps this has always been true, but we need not look far for evidence of its reality today. Just consider what our language reveals. Someone looking back at life may observe, "I have come a long way." If life seems particularly fulfilled at some moment, a person may say, "I feel like I've arrived," or "I've made it to the top of the mountain." Others regret "detours" taken along the way. Someone who feels frustrated by life may remark, "I don't feel like I'm going anywhere."

Who among us has not spoken of "crossroads" we have "come to" in our lives? Clearly our everyday conversations are filled with the language of the journey. If the episodes of our lives take place one after another, as in a story as we noted in the Introduction, these episodes also seem to be leading us somewhere, taking us forward as on a journey. From this perspective it is natural that "journey" and "story" should come together often, and that we would be drawn to these particular stories.

But perhaps these stories are pervasive also because many of us indeed sense that something is lacking or lost or inexplicable in the world around us, in our own lives, or in both, as the stories say. In all times and cultures, for example, folks have found themselves discontented with wealth and power despite the allure of these. In our particular time many of us know that science and technology, even in this technological age, will not save us. In fact, in some ways these have made life more frightening (e.g., our loss of privacy). Soelle claims that working and consuming, which have become the very essence of life in the Western world, are destroying us.[7] Many of us mourn the loss of places of natural beauty even as we share the benefits of commercial development. We often feel the tension between these deep within ourselves.

And so, today, as poverty increases despite all our economic development, as wars still break out, as families continue to break up despite all our "progress," as people clutter their lives with things they do not need, as many are stuck in jobs with no appeal to their creativity because of bills they must pay, as violence happens ever nearer all of us, as we witness the damage done to our environment, as decency and dignity seem to decline, many are those who feel deeply unsettled in their lives. They yearn for what Soelle calls "wholeness and soundness," for a "life that is not fragmented," that is "free of calculation and fear." They yearn to be able to trust, hope, believe, and love, to be "at home" in themselves.[8] In the language of this book, these unsettled ones yearn to be authentically human, to be fully the persons God created them to be. Many of us have learned along with pilgrims of old that the world "out there" does not lead us "home." Yet we often don't know where else to turn. The ethos of our technological, consumer age discourages attention to the inner world, as spirituality teacher Joan Chittister has observed: "Western culture has tied the definition of adulthood to the ability to achieve. So we spend our lives getting education or money or things or status. As a result we are inclined to forget the need for inner development."[9] Psychologist Ronald D. Laing concurs: "Our world is so alien to the inner world that many people insist that the inner world does not exist at all, and if it does exist, it makes no difference."[10] But this is not true in the stories. Particularly not the journey stories.

So in all times and continuing today, unsettled folk who are looking beyond the world "out there" and who hear or read these *good* stories seriously can recognize in them an "essential something." The stories offer a new way of seeing, being, and valuing in the world that rings true, that can answer our deepest yearnings for authenticity and show us the way home. Psychology of Religion Professor Edward Thornton relates an incident at a bed and breakfast in which he told the other guests there (when they discovered he was a professor on a sabbatical leave and asked about his work) that in Dante's *The Comedy* he "had discovered a story that helps make sense out of life. Their response was excited and positive. Their hunger for what I described was acute."[11] Here, then, is a major reason such stories are so pervasive: For hundreds and hundreds of years they have helped people make sense of their lives in ways the external world never can, for they lead people on a spiritual journey, a journey of the soul to become the persons God created them to be. They are still doing that.

All the above leads to what may now seem an obvious conclusion: These *good* stories teach us that attending to our spiritual journeys is a necessary part of becoming authentically human. Now we who are Christian may wonder about our sacred stories—what do they say about this matter? I am glad you asked! We find one answer to this question by pursuing another one: What if Mark's gospel could be, or even should be, read as a journey story? Might we learn something about attending to the journey of our souls from this gospel story?

The Journey Story in Mark's Gospel

The initial hint that Mark may be read as a journey story comes in the opening prophecy Mark quotes. Twice the prophecy announces that God sends a messenger to "prepare *the way* [*hodos*] of the Lord" (1:2–3). The Greek word *hodos* may be translated as way or road or journey. It can denote a literal, physical road or metaphorically designate the course of a life. Scholars have long noted that from this beginning, "the way" becomes a verbal thread running throughout the gospel, giving thematic structure to the story (readers can check such verses as 6:8; 8:27; 9:33–34; 10:32; 10:52). So New Testament scholar Werner Kelber describes Jesus in Mark as being in "constant movement from place to place, from region to region, frequently back and forth, and all the way from life to death. Jesus' whole career is conceived in Mark as a journey."[12] But he is not only moving across the physical landscape of first-century Palestine. Being "on the way" also means that Jesus is moving toward God.[13]

Despite these helpful observations about "the way" and Jesus' journey in Mark, scholars have not read this gospel either as a journey story like the ones just discussed or alongside these kinds of journey stories in order to see what they might see.[14] That's what I propose that we do now.

A Disruption

A journey story begins in a world in which something drives people beyond its confines and disturbs and disrupts the sense that everything is "beautiful and perfect." Everything seems fine, and then it doesn't.[15] Jumping Mouse was "busy as all mice are, busy with mice things," until the day he heard the roar of the river in his ears and had to know what that roar was. Frodo was enjoying being master of his hobbit hole at Bag End in the Shire in Middle-earth. Then Gandalf the wizard showed up to tell him that the Ring his Uncle Bilbo had bequeathed him was the One Ring of power that the evil lord Sauron was seeking. And John the Baptizer appeared in the Judean wilderness preaching repentance and baptizing people in the Jordan River (Mark 1:4).

John looked and acted like a prophet, like the great prophet Elijah in fact, whom God was to send as a messenger before "the great and terrible day of the LORD" (see Mal. 3:1–2; 4:5–6). Mark says that *all* the people of Judea and Jerusalem went out to him (1:5)–hyperbole, no doubt (we can hardly imagine the great city of Jerusalem literally vacant), but it makes the point that something extraordinary was happening. A disturbing, disrupting moment had occurred in their world. A prophet like Elijah was calling the people to repent, that is, telling them the way they were traveling was no longer taking them to God. So, like Dante, they must go by another road. The familiar and expected path would not do. John also said, "One is coming after me who is stronger than me...I baptized you with water but he will baptize you with the Holy Spirit" (1:7–8). We expect that this Coming One will show us the other way, the different way, the way of the Lord.

The Summons

According to the stories, the "Coming One" must now be summoned. So indeed Jesus came from Nazareth in Galilee–a journey in itself–and was baptized by John (1:9). At this point in the story this occurrence is quite ordinary. Jesus is baptized like the others who came to hear John. Sensitive readers, however, can feel the "but" that is coming. "*But* as he was *coming up* from the water he saw…" Let me interrupt my translation of Mark's text (the emphases are mine too) to point out that what follows is Jesus' own experience. We are not told that John or anyone else who may have been present saw what happened. We are only told that *Jesus* saw "the heavens being torn open and the Spirit as a dove *coming down* into him" (1:10). An auditory experience then follows the visual: "a voice from heaven happened: 'you are my son the beloved; in you I am well pleased'" (1:11). This experience is also Jesus' own as the words "*you are* my son" indicate (compare Mt. 3:17). In Mark's telling, this event was not a grand announcement to many people, but a significant moment for Jesus.

How might we understand the content of this vision Jesus sees and hears? The heavens were thought to be a great cosmic curtain separating creation from God's presence, but the heavens in Mark's story are torn open, even ripped apart. The Greek verb is a strong, almost violent word. Interpreters have long thought this tearing of the heavens means human beings have new access to God. But maybe it also signals that God will no longer be confined to sacred spaces–where we human beings often try to lock God away–but is on the loose in our realm.[16] So we should not be surprised that when the heavens were torn open, the Spirit came down like a dove into Jesus. God is up to something! Now we can note the movement in this text, for it may be telling: As Jesus "comes up" (the Greek word is *anabaino*) from the water, the Spirit "comes down" (the Greek word is *katabaino*) into Jesus. Maybe we are to understand the divine voice of approval in verse 11 as the result of Jesus' having "risen" to meet the challenge, so to speak. He has answered the summons to join with God in whatever God is up to.

Aid for the Journey, and the First Threshold

The stories now tell us that those who answer the summons are given spiritual guides for their journeys. In the fairy tale "The Golden Bird" a wise fox is there to tell the king's sons where to go, what to do, and what to avoid. Frodo has Gandalf the wizard. Dante's Pilgrim has the great Roman poet Virgil as teacher and guide. And Jesus has the Spirit, who has come down into him from the heavens. The Spirit's guidance of Jesus begins immediately after Jesus' baptism and summons when the Spirit "drove him out into the wilderness" (1:12).

We might well wonder if Jesus thought he could do without guidance that drove him into the wilderness! We might even wonder about the Greek verb translated in the NRSV as "*drove* him," which can also mean "*threw* him out there." Is this forceful verb a hint that Jesus did not want to go into the wilderness? If so, who can blame him? Few of us dream of time alone in a dry desert where wild animals are! And yet, the stories tell us that after saying yes to a summons, a difficult moment comes soon that tells the journeying one that the road, though it promises to lead to "paradise," will not be easy. This threshold symbolizes the resistance—both internal fears and external pressures—encountered by anyone who leaves the ordinary world for a risky journey into the unknown.[17] Standing on the threshold, the pilgrim must decide if he or she will cross over and stay on the journey or turn back.

The king in "The Golden Bird" sent first his eldest and then his second son on a journey to find the special bird. When neither returned, he reluctantly sent his youngest son. Like his brothers, the youngest son encountered a fox who gave this counsel: Soon he would come to two inns, one "lighted up brightly and with all sorts of amusement and gaiety going on," and the other "dark and dismal." He must stay in the dark inn, said the fox. We readers know the first two sons stayed in the bright inn and, "living only a life of pleasure and luxury," remained there and quit the journey. The third son, however, passed the night in the dark inn and the next morning, having crossed the first threshold, set out again.[18]

When John Bunyan's pilgrim began his journey, he had a companion. But they soon fell into a miry bog called the "Slough of Despond" in which they "wallowed for a time, being grievously bedaubed with the dirt." At this point Christian's companion complained:

> "Is this the happiness you have told me all this while of? If we have such ill speed at our first setting out, what may we expect between this and our journey's end? May I get out again with my life, you shall possess the brave country alone for me." And with that, he gave a desperate struggle or two, and got out of the mire on the side of the slough which was

next to his own house: so away he went, and Christian saw him no more.[19]

With "spiritual help," Christian got out on the other side of the bog. Having crossed his first threshold, he continued his journey.

Instead of a miry bog, Jesus (in Mark's story) encounters his first threshold in the wilderness, driven there by the Spirit for forty days. For Jesus himself, as well as for those reading Mark's story, there would have been great associations with "wilderness." As a literal place the biblical tradition views it as land that is wide-open space, unsurveyed, unmapped, undomesticated by human beings. It is still free of human control. It may even appear to us as wasted and empty. So it became the primary scriptural symbol of the absence of human aid and comfort and, consequently, a deepened awareness of human reliance on God. If God had not provided a way through the Red Sea, manna each morning, water from a rock, the cloud by day, and the pillar of fire by night, the children of Israel would not have survived their forty-year journey through the wilderness to the promised land. If angels had not provided food and water for Elijah, his forty-day pilgrimage to Horeb to encounter God's presence in the silence (the famous "still, small voice") would have been too much for him (1 Kings 19).

A few hundred years after Jesus, his followers turned to the wilderness again to move beyond the lives and control of other human beings and renew their awareness of God. Beginning with Saint Anthony of Egypt (251–356) these first monks retreated to the desert to confront and be healed of their "passions." By the term "passions" the monks were not referring merely to strong emotions (as we use the term today). Instead, they were concerned with thoughts, feelings, and ways of seeing or acting that hindered love of God and neighbor. To confront the passions, therefore, was to confront the demonic within themselves. So the way into the wilderness inevitably led to what they described as spiritual warfare, that is, the sense of being tempted by Satan as Jesus was. They required spiritual discernment to discover where healing and renewal lay. The end result for those who did not turn back from the journey into the desert was purity of heart, a unified vision of God, and a deep sense of purpose in their lives.[20]

Similarly, native peoples have always had those among them who journey beyond the margins of society, into the wilderness, on vision quests. While they travel deep into the wilderness, they are simultaneously journeying inward, seeking purification and self-encounter in order to discover the identity and destiny of their people. The difficult overland journey into the wilderness and the more difficult journey in the spirit are together necessary for a new vision.[21]

In Mark's story Jesus is the one in the wilderness. Driven there by the Spirit, he is tempted by Satan for forty days and is with the wild beasts (1:13). Many readers of Mark automatically add in their own minds the explicit temptations given by Matthew and Luke. I suspect, however, that Mark hoped we might think along different lines. The associations with Israel's forty-year sojourn in the wilderness and Elijah's forty days of travel to Horeb call to mind those who were tempted to quit the journey. Under a solitary broom tree one day's journey into the wilderness Elijah moaned, "It is enough; now, O LORD, take away my life" (1 Kings 19:4). As the children of Israel feared first Pharaoh's army, then no food, then no water, they complained to Moses, "Is it because there are no graves in Egypt that you have taken us out to die in the wilderness? What is this that you have done to us, bringing us out of Egypt? Is this not the very word that we spoke to you in Egypt, saying: Let us alone that we may serve Egypt! Indeed better for us serving Egypt than our dying in the wilderness!" (Ex. 14:11–12).[22]

These stories from the Hebrew Bible, along with other journey stories, suggest we would do well to understand that in the wilderness in Mark, Jesus faced deep resistance to his journey and was tempted to turn back from the way to which he had been called. Even the strange reference to the wild beasts may serve this purpose if the beasts symbolize the dangers Jesus faced as he followed the Spirit's guidance, as many believe.[23] Thus, we see that after the great high of the baptism moment comes the stark reality that the way of the Lord is a difficult journey. It involves spiritual warfare and even danger as the stories, the scriptures, and also the desert fathers and mothers have taught us. So Jesus has encountered his first threshold. Will he journey on, or will he turn back?

Beginning the Road of Trials

Mark does not narrate an explicit answer to this question. But since the next we hear of Jesus he has returned to Galilee and is preaching the gospel of God (1:14), we know from the unfolding story that he crossed this first threshold and continued onward. So, we may wonder, how did he find the courage to go on? The answer is twofold, the first part of which may be rather obvious. Just as Christian got spiritual help getting out of the Slough of Despond and the angels took care of Elijah, so Mark tells us the angels ministered to Jesus (1:13). The way of the Lord is indeed difficult. Neither the stories nor Mark try to soften the difficult realities of the spiritual journey. But the stories and Mark also promise spiritual aid for the journey. As Soelle has noted, the way is not restricted to the exceptionally gifted or heroic folk among us. All kinds of people have heard a summons from God, and *with God's help* have continued the journey to which they have been called.[24]

The second part of the answer to how Jesus found the courage to continue is suggested to us by Dante. Dante's description of hell includes a famous inscription on the gate at the entrance. The inscription reads: "Abandon hope all you who enter here." Dante's story shows us that the decisive factor in continuing the journey or turning back is hope versus the abandoning of hope. Hope has its roots in faith that the journey is going somewhere, that "paradise" is "out there," and the way we are traveling will take us there.[25]

So let us note Jesus' words as he comes out of his wilderness experience: "The time is fulfilled and the *basileia*[26] of God has drawn near" (1:15). The Greek verb for "has drawn" is perfect tense, which presents an action that has already taken place but with effects that continue to have an impact. Western Protestant Christianity has tended to focus on the future dimension of Jesus' message of the *basileia* (see, e.g., Mark 8:38; 13:24–27). In so doing we have diluted the force of the perfect tense verb in 1:15. Well, let the diluting stop! Mark has previously told us that the heavens were torn open so that God would be on the loose in our world (1:10). God's dramatic irruption into our space necessarily means that changes are *now* underway. God's eschatological activity in the world (i.e., drawing the *basileia* near) is underway even in the midst of the old ways that have not yet passed on. God's new age does not await a future, cataclysmic event to be launched–it *has drawn* near!

Thus, Jesus proclaimed to the people of his day that they need no longer live under Caesar's rule, for the *basileia* of GOD is present and available for them! Reaching into our own time is the implication that the injustices, oppression, exploitation, and suffering created by the self-serving human ordering of life is not the only reality in the world, for God has brought God's own *basileia* near to us. As Mark's story unfolds, we will discover that the present dimension of

God's *basileia* involves a whole new way of being together as God's people in the power of the Spirit, who guides us on the Way. Here is reason to hope, therefore, and hope enables the journey! So Jesus journeyed through Galilee saying, "repent," that is, go this new Way of the Lord because God's *basileia* has drawn near, but the old ways will not take us there.

So This Is a Journey Story!

In fifteen verses Mark has given us a narrative that reads like the beginning of a journey story. We have in John's preaching a rupture in the way things have been in the world. There is a summons to Jesus and spiritual aid granted him for the way he must go. He crossed a first threshold in the wilderness. We found a sense of the hope that carried him forward. The rest of the second gospel also reads well as a journey story, but since I will be treating many of those moments along Mark's "way of the Lord" in the following chapters, I hope readers will be satisfied for now with the following few points to show a journey story pattern in the rest of Mark.

First, and perhaps most obviously, Jesus continues his constant movement "from place to place, from region to region, frequently back and forth, and all the way from life to death" as we noted earlier in the quote from Kelber. For the first eight chapters he moves around and just beyond Galilee before journeying steadily to Jerusalem to confront the chief authorities in the holiest of cities. Second, journey stories are always about a "road of trials." Would any of us doubt that Jesus travels such a road? The religious authorities plot his death from the third chapter onward. They challenge him publicly to try to dishonor him before the people and thus prevent any opposition to their death plot against him. Then there are his bumbling disciples, who try him sorely along the way. Third, journey stories have "belly of the whale" or "dark night of the soul" moments wherein the pilgrim's very life is on the line. Would any of us doubt that Jesus goes there? Would Gethsemane qualify? Would the crucifixion with Jesus' cry, "My God, my God, why have you forsaken me?" Surely so.

So I hope that this treatment of Mark 1:1–15 and these hints about the rest of Mark's story justify my belief that Mark may be read, perhaps even should be read, as a journey story. Reading Mark from this perspective yields new insights into the text itself. But there is still more that we may glean from this reading.

The Journey in Mark and the Human Condition

We noted at the beginning of this chapter that journey stories are fundamentally about inner journeys. Every feeling or impulse, every turning point in a life, every spiritual experience or insight is contained in these stories, though they are depicted as outward objects or actions. For those who feel unsettled in their lives and yearn to be "at home" within themselves, *good* journey stories can have a transforming effect. They call us away from the world "out there" to discover the deepest needs and longings within us. In our time the stories call us away from the external world of science and technology, of producing and consuming, of outward objects and actions as answers to life's most probing questions, so that we may attend to the journey of our souls to God. When we read Mark's gospel through this journey lens, it can be such a story for us. Yes, Mark gives us important historical information about Jesus and the early church. Yes, Mark gives us important information about the theology and christology of the first Christians. But also Mark's story can be for us a *good* journey story that gives guidance for our own spiritual journeys as it shows us "the way of the Lord." In so doing it can help us be more authentically human.

The obvious question now is, what specific direction does Mark as a journey story offer us? Much of what will comprise a full answer to this question can only be given after treating the gospel more broadly over the next chapters of this book. But we are able, even after closely examining only the first fifteen verses of the gospel, to see some of the guidance Mark offers about being authentically human.

First, and probably fundamentally, Mark, along with other journey stories, opens to us the ancient wisdom that sees all of life as a spiritual journey. Those who have not viewed their lives in this way are encouraged by *good* stories to do so. In George MacDonald's 1867 fairy tale *The Golden Key,* Mossy and Tangle journey to find the door that their golden key opens. When they find and open it, they discover a "winding stair within" that takes them on their next journey to the "country whence the shadows fall," which is "home" for them. In this story the end of a journey is the beginning of another—a vivid portrayal of the significance of "journey" in the lives of those who are authentically human.

Mark's story likewise invites readers on a spiritual journey. Immediately after crossing his first threshold and beginning the "road of trials," Jesus encountered Simon, Andrew, James, and John and said to them, "Follow me" (1:16–20). Thus, Mark calls us to attend to the journey of our souls by following Jesus on the "Way of the Lord." Mark offers us great grace by inviting us to see life this way. Such a view of our lives allows us to count on ourselves and others to have traveled part of the way, but not to expect either ourselves or others to have "arrived" yet. Each of us has experience and wisdom to share. Each of us also has faults not yet perfected, wounds not yet healed, and sins not yet confessed, because our journeys are not complete. Thus, the journey image allows us a realistic awareness of where we are in life so that we think neither too highly nor too lowly of ourselves or others as we all travel along the way. This realistic awareness of ourselves and others is what spiritual masters intend when they urge us to humility if we would be the persons God created us to be.[27]

Second, Mark joins other *good* journey stories in guiding us to believe that ruptures in our lives—whether the result of internal yearnings or of external circumstances that make us question where we are headed—and consequent decisions to travel "another road" are not (necessarily) signs that we have lost our minds. Such ruptures may well open us to a summons from God to a new way of living and being in the world. Mark and the stories tell us that all pilgrims experience them, which suggests, of course, that opening ourselves to such ruptures and the resulting sense of call are part of being authentically human. Now please know that I am not saying that God sends such things as dreaded illnesses or disasters such as flooding or war so as to summon someone to the spiritual journey. Some disruptions in life are only about pain, and God is not their cause. There are disturbances, however, that cause us to become aware that all is not well with our current direction in life. Sometimes this awareness comes as the result of external events. I know, for example, of folks unjustly fired from jobs who later said they knew the job did not fit their lives, but they ignored that awareness out of fear of trying something new. Being fired freed them finally to listen to what their spirits sensed about their lives and to seek a new way for themselves.

Some of us who choose "another road" need the reassurance of the stories when family and friends are sure we have lost our minds. The stories tell us that others often thought pilgrims were "not playing with a full deck." Frodo's sense that he could not always remain in the Shire led many to question his "hobbit-sense," as "to the amazement of sensible folk he was sometimes seen far from home walking in the hills and woods under the starlight."[28] The relatives of Bunyan's pilgrim, Christian, "thought that some frenzy distemper had got into his head; therefore, it drawing toward night, and they hoping that sleep might settle his brains, with all haste they got him to bed."[29] Even Jesus' family thought him mad (Mark 3:21). Just because others thought them crazy did not make it so, however. The stories make plain that the summons they had heard was genuinely from God.

Despite the pain and fear of the disruption for many, and despite intimates thinking them mad, those choosing to be authentically human, or (as Mark says) those believing that the *basileia* of God has drawn near, make the journey "there" as God shows them the way. Here I could relate any number of other kinds of stories. These are not ancient tales, but contemporary stories of former classmates, of seminary students I teach now, and of friends who have made a drastic change of direction at some point in their lives in response to a summons to something more. The former librarian at the seminary where I teach, a man in his fifties who had been at the seminary ten years, left his position with us to pursue ministry and ordination through a chaplaincy program. Although we grieved his leaving us, how could we not respect and celebrate his yes to the summons he had heard? A friend in mid-life ceased her private psychotherapy practice, sold her large Victorian house, put most of her belongings in storage, and moved into a two-room dormitory suite at a seminary in another city because of her sense of God's call. Any seminary in the country is filled with students with similar stories.[30]

But let me hasten to add that not all calls from God are to go to seminary! Others have changed careers in other directions, simplified their lives significantly, altered relationships, begun to pray when before they had not, and so on. My own biggest "rupture" came earlier in life than happens for many (when I had less at stake than friends just mentioned, though at the time it seemed quite wrenching to me). All through high school and my early college years I was intent on becoming a journalist. While high school classmates "tried on" many career possibilities and college friends fretted about major courses of study, which they changed repeatedly, I was sure of my future. Until I was hit one day in a journalism course by the proverbial ton of bricks—the realization that I did not want to do this for a living. Months of soul-searching followed before I admitted what seemed just short of impossible in the late 1970s: I (a woman) had a deep sense of God's call to ministry as my vocation. I would love to have a nickel for every friend at the time who said to me, "Sure, you don't want to be a journalist, so come to law school with me." Twenty years later I smile at the memory and at the grace-filled, difficult road that has unfolded for me. Many can give witness that Mark and the stories are right: The ruptures, the summons, and saying yes to the summons have enabled us to be more authentically human, more the persons God created us to be.

Third, Mark guides us to see that "wilderness" experiences, times when our spirits and souls seem dry, arid, and empty while "wild beasts" roam near, do not mean that God has abandoned us. Nor do they mean (necessarily) that we have lost our way. The heaven-sent guide for Dante first leads him straight into hell. Sayadio had to journey to the "land of the spirits" (i.e., the place of the dead) to find his sister's spirit. Bunyan's Christian "must needs go through [the Valley of the Shadow of Death], because the way to the Celestial City lay through the midst of it. Now this valley is a very solitary place...a wilderness, a land of deserts and pits, a land of drought...where no [one] dwelt."[31] In Mark's story the Spirit that came down into Jesus from heaven is the very reason Jesus was in the wilderness—the Spirit "drove" him there.

There is a strain of spiritual teaching out and about today that church historian Martin Marty has described as a "foot-stomping, exuberant" teaching that has "the abundant life of sunshine and joy" as its goal. Marty calls this a "summer spirituality." It shouts "the language of abundance and life" and presents the ways of the Lord in easy explanations that cause "shadowless joy" to burst into one's heart.[32] Similarly, I once heard a popular Christian writer and speaker tell a congregation of seminary students that they had no right ever to be down or depressed because "they may not know what the future holds, but they know who holds the future." Well, the stories disagree. So do the desert fathers and mothers who told of the spiritual warfare they encountered in their desire to become pure of heart. So does Mark's gospel.

This first threshold experience will cause many to turn back from the journey when they realize that "sunshine and shadowless joy" are not the only realities they will face on the Way. Theirs is an unfortunate choice, for wilderness experiences are necessary stages on the journey for those who seek to be authentically human. These dry and difficult moments are ones that force us to ask ourselves such questions as, Why am I here? Because I am seeking God, or because of some other reason that is primarily about my ego? Mark tells us about many who hear "the word" and "immediately receive it with joy." But they have no root in themselves but are capricious as the weather, so when tribulation or persecution on account of the word happens, immediately they turn away" (4:16–17). Or maybe we find ourselves finally asking ourselves honestly: Is there some resistance within me that is preventing me from journeying forward? Note the following "wilderness" story (it actually takes place in a cave) from the early monastic movement:

> A brother was restless in the community and often moved to anger. So he said, "I will go, and live somewhere by myself. And since I shall be able to talk or listen to no one, I shall be tranquil, and my passionate anger will cease." He went out and lived alone in a cave. But one day he filled his jug with water and put it on the ground. It happened suddenly to fall over. He filled it again, and again it fell. And this happened a third time. And in a rage he snatched up the jug and broke it. Returning to his right mind, he knew that the demon of anger had mocked him, and he said…"I will return to the community. Wherever you live, you need effort and patience and above all God's help."[33]

So in these ways and others, wilderness experiences, with their "aridities and trials," are actually "an inflowing of God into the soul." They purge and cleanse the hearts of pilgrims and prepare them for "the delectable life of love with God"[34] which is the goal of the journey. While we do not find poetic language such as this (from Saint John of the Cross) in Mark, we are given a hint that Mark believed Jesus' wilderness experience was an "inflowing of God into his soul": Jesus came out of the desert proclaiming, "The *basileia* of God has drawn near."

Finally, the stories that nudge us toward our spiritual journeys offer hope for the way. They show us a vision of a destination that is worth the trials of the journey, and they promise spiritual guidance as we travel. Dante's story, in fact, says that those who abandon hope never get to paradise but are stuck in hell. Having lost hope in God's way, they choose deceit, manipulation, violence, betrayal, and so forth to get their own ego-centered way. Their "reward" is to reap for eternity the natural consequences of their choices. This is their hell. Mark's story does not explicitly mention hope, as Dante does, but it surely offers its own hopeful vision of "paradise": The *basileia* of God has drawn near! The rest of the gospel will unpack what that means for Jesus and followers of Jesus and show us the way "there," that is, how to share in it. Here at the beginning of Mark the hope of living in God's *basileia* rather than Caesar's for Mark's first readers, or rather than under Western cultural definitions of success and achievement (one example of tyranny for many of us today) can spur us to begin the journey.

Furthermore, Mark's story concurs with the other stories by showing us we can hope for spiritual guidance along the way. The Spirit who came down into Jesus at his baptism immediately became Jesus' guide, as we see when it drove him into the wilderness. Again, we may initially smile a rueful smile and think that that is guidance we could do without. But such is not true. All the stories, including Mark's, tell us that the way to paradise, to the *basileia* of God, to being authentically human, goes through the wilderness. Were it not for the Spirit's guidance we might never choose on our own to go that way, which means we would never arrive at the destinations for which we hope. Even Jesus had to be "driven" there by the Spirit. So the Spirit's guidance is essential. Mark promises it for all who follow the Way of the Lord: Not only does the Spirit come down into Jesus but John had earlier proclaimed that when the Coming One (Jesus) arrived, he would baptize others in the Spirit (1:8). Those who would be authentically human, therefore, open themselves in hope to the Spirit's guidance on the Way of the Lord to the *basileia* of God.

Concluding Thoughts

People of all times, places, and cultures have told journey stories. Outwardly these are stories about particular folks traveling "overland" and having adventures on the way. Fundamentally, however, they are about inner journeys people take in search of "paradise," to find wholeness and soundness in their lives, to enter the *basileia* of God. When interpreters "translate" these stories into such journeys of the soul, they become transformative guides offering aid to pilgrims who are seeking to become more authentically human.

Mark's gospel may be read as such a journey story. Like the other stories, it begins with a disruption in the way life has been when John calls people to repent. It has a summons to the "Coming One" (Jesus) who can lead people on a new way. There is the gift of spiritual guidance for the journey, a first threshold Jesus must cross in the wilderness experience, and hope for the journey in the announcement that the *basileia* of God has drawn near. The rest of the gospel also reads well as a journey story, but Mark's beginning seems a particularly clear invitation to read this story this way.

When we do so, Mark becomes a transformative guide for us on our inner journeys. Especially for those of us who are Christian, Mark's gospel (as one of our sacred stories) gives guidance as we follow Jesus on the journey. It calls us to follow the Way of the Lord as Jesus travels it and encourages and reassures us about experiences of rupture in our lives along with a sense of summons or call from God. It promises us spiritual guidance along the way–Mark's story tells us Jesus baptizes followers in the same Spirit who came upon him at his baptism and guided him on his journey. The story does not promise that the journey will be all sunshine and joy, however. There are thresholds to cross, wildernesses to encounter, spiritual warfare to endure. To pass through these experiences under guidance from the Spirit rather than avoiding them is to travel the Way of the Lord, according to Mark. Why should we travel this way, then, if it is difficult? Because, Mark shows us, it leads us into the *basileia* of God, which is not only a future possibility. It is the hope of a new way of being in the world now, a way of being authentically human, a way of coming home to ourselves.

Let the journey begin.

CHAPTER 2

"SEE WHAT YOU HEAR!"
(Mark 4:24)

THE GREAT RABBI JOSHUA BEN LEVI was certain that all his knowledge of Torah and Talmud did not give him the wisdom for life that he sought, so he prayed for Elijah to come to teach him. When Elijah came, he said Rabbi Joshua could travel with him but not ask questions or voice comments along the way. Their journey was unusual: they stayed with a kind, poor farmer couple, after which Elijah prayed that their one prize cow would die; they visited a greedy, uncompassionate rich man, after which Elijah miraculously rebuilt a crumbling wall for the man so that it would stand for generations; they entered a rude and arrogant town for which Elijah prayed that everyone there would become a leader; they came to a small village of kind and generous people for whom Elijah prayed there would be only one leader. At this point Rabbi Joshua could be silent no longer and exploded with his demands to know the meaning of Elijah's strange actions. Elijah then explained: he knew the first farmer was to die the next day and asked that the cow die instead; under the rich man's wall was a chest of gold—now that the wall was rebuilt so sturdily, the rich man would never find the chest and reap its benefits; a community with too many leaders will argue and be discontent until they change their arrogant ways, while a village with one strong leader will grow and prosper— hence the prayers for the two towns. Then Elijah said, "Rabbi Joshua...You say you wish for the keys to wisdom and understanding of life on earth. The first key to wisdom is to realize that all that you see is not what it seems."[1]

ONCE UPON A TIME, shortly after the second time Jesus fed a multitude of people despite scarce resources, as he and his disciples were crossing the sea of Galilee in a boat, he said to them, "Look, see the yeast of the Pharisees and of Herod!" The disciples didn't get it. They said to each other, "It must be because we haven't enough bread with us." Jesus overheard them and said, "Why are you talking about having no bread? Do you still not understand? Having eyes, do you not see? When I broke the five loaves for the five thousand, how many baskets of broken pieces did you gather?" They answered, "Twelve." "And the seven for the four thousand, how many baskets of broken pieces did you gather?" They answered, "Seven." And he said, "Don't you get it?" They said nothing. And they came to Bethsaida where people brought him a blind man and encouraged Jesus to touch him. Jesus took the man outside the village and spit on his eyes and laid hands on him and asked him, "Do you see anything?" The man saw something and said, "I see people, but they look like walking trees." Jesus laid hands on him again, and this time the man saw everything clearly.

MARK 8:14–26, PARAPHRASED

ONCE UPON A TIME the religious and political leaders of the day conspired to kill Jesus to end the threat he posed to them. They found him guilty of blasphemy and sedition in a kangaroo court and had him crucified. As he hung there dying, the chief priests and scribes mocked him, "He saved others but he cannot save himself. Let the messiah come down from the cross now so that we may see and believe." But the centurion guarding him, when he saw how Jesus died, said, "Truly this man was God's son."

MARK 15:31–32, 37–39, PARAPHRASED

Early in Mark's gospel, after telling a story about a sower (Mark 4:2–9), explaining it to those who were around him, including the Twelve, who did not understand (4:13–20), then encouraging them again with the benefits of "getting" his teaching (4:21–23), Jesus challenged his followers to "*See* what you hear!" (the literal translation of the Greek in 4:24a). Thus is launched a major emphasis on "seeing" in Mark's story. We find it in the episodes involving the disciples in the boat, the blind man of Bethsaida, and the centurion at the cross among others. I am intrigued by the attention given to "seeing" in Mark, not least because Elijah told Rabbi Joshua that the first key to wisdom is "to realize that all that you see is not what it seems." Furthermore, Edward Thornton insists that developing "the capacity for seeing the unseen is the key discipline for the [spiritual] journey."[2] There is surely much value for us, therefore, in attending to Mark's focus on "seeing." So in this chapter we will review the significant moments in the development of this motif in Mark. With the help of other *good* stories we will discover an interpretation as we review. The stories help us *see* Mark's theme more clearly and affirm the kind of seeing that Mark urges on us as essential for those who would be authentically human. Then, in the last part of the chapter, we will note specific reasons why the call to see, as narrated in this first-century text, matters to those of us in the twenty-first century who are committed to the journey to God.

Discovering Mark's Call to See

We should know, first, that the Greek word *blepo*, Mark's favorite choice among several words that can mean see, ordinarily denotes sense perception, that is, being able to see as distinct from physical blindness. Its simple meaning is made clear in the New Testament: It is not used for appearances of the risen Christ nor for visions of eschatological fulfillment. Indeed, it is rarely used for anything visionary at all. But let us note: It can be used figuratively.[3]

So, at Mark 4:24, after telling and interpreting parables, Jesus says, "*Blepo* [not "take heed" or "pay attention" as most translations have, but *see*] what you hear!" At 8:14–15, the moment recounted above when Jesus and some of his followers were crossing the Sea of Galilee, he challenged them, "Look, *see* [*blepo*] the yeast of the Pharisees and the yeast of Herod." "Yeast" in those days was a symbol for the evil inclinations of human beings. So Jesus' words were surely intended as a challenge to followers to recognize the evil in the actions of the religious and political leadership of the time. Throughout his ministry in Galilee these leaders had opposed his liberation of people from whatever bound their lives (rigid purity rules, demons, fear of persecution, illness, economic exploitation, etc.).[4] Thus, Jesus may have meant that these leaders' evil was their general opposition to the freedom and compassion of God that he offered. But perhaps we readers should look for their "yeast" more specifically in the immediately preceding story. There the Pharisees tested Jesus by asking for a "sign from heaven," that is, for some literal and concrete proof of his claims about God (8:11). Jesus refused their request with a deep sigh (of frustration?), as well he should. In Mark's story nothing could be more indicative of God at work than freedom and compassion.

Remarkably, the disciples respond to Jesus' call to *see* this "yeast" by being concerned that they haven't sufficient bread with them in the boat (8:14, 16). They assume the literal meaning of Jesus' word "yeast" so that they, too, as Mark portrays them, are focused on concrete things. Considering that this is their third boat trip involving a significant discussion with Jesus (note 4:35–41; 6:45–52) and the third episode involving enough bread (note 6:30–44; 8:1–10), we readers have been prepared to expect better from them. So we are hardly surprised that their puny response prompts Jesus to explode at them, "Why do you discuss that you have no bread?... Are your hearts hardened? Having eyes do you not *see* [*blepo*]?" (8:17–18).

Nor should we be surprised that the next episode in Mark's story begins, "And he came into Bethsaida. And they were bringing to him a blind man, and they were calling out to him so that he might touch him"(8:22). This story of Jesus' healing a blind person, together with the only other such story in Mark, the healing of Bartimaeus (10:46–52), serves as a "frame" for Jesus' journey to Jerusalem in Mark (8:27–10:52). During this journey he tells his followers plainly (8:32) about his destiny (Jerusalem and the cross) and invites them to follow him on that way.

In the first healing of a blind person, Jesus spit on the man's eyes, laid his hands on him, and asked him, "Do you *see* [*blepo*] anything?" (8:23). The man could indeed see, but not clearly (people looked like walking trees to him). So Jesus laid hands on him again. This time the man "looked steadily [*diablepo*] and was restored and was *seeing* [*emblepo*] everything clearly" (8:25). The story brings to mind Jesus' disciples, who see something in Jesus (after all, they are with him), but they do not see clearly what God is doing through him. They need a second touch. Jesus' plain teaching about his destiny on the way to Jerusalem may be read as his effort to "lay hands on them" again.

At the end of this journey, Jesus encountered the blind man Bartimaeus, who begged Jesus for mercy (10:47–48). When Jesus asked him what he wished Jesus would do for him, Bartimaeus replied, "Rabbi, let me *see* [*anablepo*]" (10:51). Jesus granted his request so that immediately he *saw* (*anablepo*) and followed Jesus on the way to Jerusalem and the cross (10:52).

The theme continues throughout Mark. Four times in the apocalyptic discourse in Mark 13 *see* (*blepo*) is used as an imperative (though the English translations hide them well!). One of these is in 13:9 wherein Jesus warns his followers, "*See* yourselves, for they will betray you." Note how some English versions present this verse: The NRSV has "as for yourselves, beware"; the NIV reads, "You must be on your guard"; the NAB says, "Watch out for yourselves"; while the RSV offers, "But take heed to yourselves." Not only do these translations fail to alert English readers that Mark's *seeing* motif is present again, but they may also convey a wrong sense of Jesus' challenge here. He is warning followers that they will be persecuted for being his disciples. So the simple translation "*see* yourselves," which could convey "look at yourselves and know why you are following Jesus," makes better sense than "be on guard" (i.e., "look out for the persecutors").

Chapter 13 also contains warnings in verse 33 to, "*See* [*blepo*]! Keep alert! For you do not know when the time is." Followers of Jesus should not be surprised or unprepared, caught off guard or insensitive to God's eschatological activity in the world.[5] Instead, they should *see* whenever God is at work bringing the *basileia* of God near and making it available, and they should be at work with God in this endeavor.[6]

Finally, there is the remarkable account in Mark of the centurion at the cross. Just before he comes on stage, so to speak, we encounter the religious leaders mocking Jesus with the words, "Let the messiah, the king of Israel come down now from the cross so that we may see and believe" (15:32). He did not come down, of course. Instead, we are introduced to the centurion who was standing guard over Jesus. Following details about Jesus' loud cry and last breath, and the temple curtain's being torn in two from top to bottom, Mark writes, "But when the centurion…*saw* that in this way he breathed his last, he said, 'Truly this man was God's son'" (15:39).[7]

I always want to ask when I get to this moment in Mark's story, What does the centurion see? What connection does he see between the way Jesus died and Jesus' being God's son? Certainly the link was not some concrete demonstration that he witnessed with his physical eyes such as the religious leaders claimed would cause them to believe (as some of them had sought in 8:11 when they asked Jesus for a sign). When we understand that there is something more than physical sight involved, we are beginning to understand the call to *see* that Mark's story issues.

Interpreting a Motif: Insightfulness

Indeed, the initial call to see in the gospel, "See what you hear!" cannot mean physical sight. We cannot literally see what we hear (we are not like comic strip characters whose words appear in bubbles near their heads). This pattern holds throughout the gospel. Jesus did not ask his followers to see actual yeast. Mark's telling of the Bartimaeus story says that when Bartimaeus is able to see, the first thing he does is follow Jesus on his way to Jerusalem and the cross. There is a connection between Jesus' death and awareness that he is God's son that is not literal or concrete, but that the centurion nonetheless sees.

Clearly, therefore, when Mark's story calls people to see, the type of sight intended is more than physical sight. It is more than our habitual seeing, more than the ordinary perception that gets us through a day at home but is inadequate for comprehending out-of-the-ordinary moments.[8] It's the kind of sight possessed by an old rabbi who had become so blind that he could neither read nor see the faces of those who visited him. A faith healer came to him and told him, "Entrust yourself to my care, and I will heal your blindness." But the rabbi said, "There will be no need for that. I can see everything I need to."[9]

We might call this sight recognition, or discernment, or insight. The great mystics speak of awareness or of being awake. Sometimes we refer to the eyes of our hearts, or of our souls, or of our spirits when we want to denote this kind of sight. It's the kind of sight we mean when we exclaim, "Oh, I see!"

And Mark harps on this theme. In addition to the texts already noted and the ones we will yet take up, we might have examined 5:30–31; 6:34; 9:1; 12:28–34. Clearly this theme was important for this storyteller. What, then, does Mark wish us "to get" about seeing, about being insightful? Other *good* stories help us.

What We See Is Not Always True

One thing the stories tell us is this: *that which we see (with our physical eyes) is not always true or real.* Just consider: Frogs certainly do not appear able to be handsome princes. Who encounters ugly ducklings and sees beautiful swans in the making? We do not usually look for heroes among the likes of the boy Arthur who removed the sword Excalibur from the stone, or Quasimodo the hunchback of Notre Dame. Indeed, Disney's version of this Victor Hugo classic begins with the narrator, the gypsy Clopin, asking the riddle, "Who is the monster and who is the man?" The question is a riddle because Claude Frollo, the minister of justice in the story, appears to be the man and the hunchbacked Quasimodo the monster. But the opposite, in fact, is true.

And of course there is the story of Elijah and Rabbi Joshua ben Levi, with which I began this chapter, which tells us that all that we see is not what it seems. In another of the Elijah stories of Jewish tradition, Elijah dressed in the rags of a beggar and knocked at the door of a home where a wedding was underway. When the father of the bride opened the door, Elijah asked if there was room at the party for one like him. The man slammed the door in Elijah's face. Then, in the fine garb of a gentleman, Elijah tried again and was welcomed. So he entered the house, went over to the table, and stuffed food into his vest and shirt and poured wine over his clothes. When the host came rushing over, demanding an explanation, Elijah said:

> When I, Elijah, came to your house in the rags of a beggar,
> I was refused entry. When I, the same Elijah, came to your
> house in the clothes of a gentleman, I was admitted. I could
> only conclude that you invited my clothes to the feast. So, I
> have proceeded to feed them.[10]

To judge Elijah by his clothes (i.e., what he "appeared" to be) was not to *see* Elijah at all.

If we pay close attention to Mark and work a bit backward in the story, we can understand that Mark matches the perspective of these stories. Earlier I mentioned that "see" is an imperative four times in the apocalyptic discourse in Mark 13, and I treated two of those. Both of the other uses of *see* are linked with "do not be deceived." In 13:5 Jesus warns followers to *see* and not be deceived by those claiming to be the Christ or saying that wars, earthquakes, or famines are signs that the end is here (vv. 6–8). In 13:22–23, Jesus cautions disciples against false messiahs and false prophets who will even do signs and wonders in order to deceive them. "But *see*! I have told all these things to you beforehand," Jesus says to them.

The episode that immediately precedes the apocalyptic discourse is the story we often call "the widow with the two mites" (12:41–44). I understand the story not to be about great faith, however, but about a widow robbed of her last two cents by a corrupt temple system.[11] That episode is "set up" by Jesus' warning just prior to it to "*see* [*blepo*] the scribes" who love to wear religious clothing and sit in the best seats so that they appear very pious (12:38–40). All the while, however, they are making long prayers only for pretense. And they devour widows' houses, either because they are embezzling from widows' estates over which they have been made trustees or because of the general injustice of the temple economic system of which they are a part.[12] These are hardly the actions of genuinely pious people.

Indeed, all the confrontations between Jesus and the religious leaders in Jerusalem (11:26–12:44) are "set up" by his cursing of the temple in 11:15–17. Mark reveals Jesus' reason for cursing the temple by framing it with the odd story of the cursing of the fig tree (11:12–14, 20–25). The fig tree is in leaf and looks good, but is not—it has no fruit (v. 13). Likewise, the temple looks beautiful on the outside (see 13:1). But note what is happening inside: There are buyers and sellers, money changers, people selling doves, and others carrying stuff through the temple (11:15–16).

Scholars using social science methods of study believe these merchants and money changers were the "street-level" representatives of Palestine's redistribution economy. In this kind of economic system goods and services are gathered into a central storehouse. The "public relations" folks say the goods will be redistributed to those in need. In reality, the leaders make sure redistribution serves their interests. Thus, in Palestine the Jerusalem temple was the central storehouse for an excessive burden of tributes, taxes, tithes, and other debts that were controlled by the religious leaders in collaboration with the Herodians and Rome. The system was so unjust that it took that widow's last two coins (12:41–44). Peasants were sometimes forced to sell their lands and even their family members into debt slavery to pay their temple taxes.[13] The temple may have looked like a house of prayer for all nations, but do not be deceived, Mark says. It had become a den of robbers (11:17).

Notice that our examination of these texts unveils Mark's portrayal of those who do evil and the evil they do as deceptive: The temple was beautiful, scribes appeared religious, and false prophets did signs and wonders. Indeed, that which we see (with our physical eyes) is not always true or real! Here our storyteller is affirming an idea found not only in other *good* stories but also elsewhere in the New Testament. John the Revelator wrote of "the great dragon, the ancient serpent, the one who is called the devil and Satan, the one who deceives the whole world" (Rev. 12:9; he repeats the idea in 13:14; 18:23; 19:20; and 20:10). Paul said that Satan disguises himself as an angel of light (2 Cor. 11:14). John records Jesus calling the devil "a liar and the father of lies" (Jn. 8:44).

A kind of logic exists in this portrayal of evil by Mark and others. Were someone to stand on a street corner and cry out, "I am evil! Follow me!" almost no one, not even the most nonreligious of people, would follow. Were the PR folks to promote an activity or program as accomplishing evil, almost no one would participate. And yet, many of us feel that evil abounds. How else could it do so except that it deceives people into not recognizing it for what it is? Therefore, with great passion and good reason Mark's story calls readers again and again to *see*. Neither people nor institutions nor circumstances may actually be as they appear.

What We Don't See May Be Most True

Other stories teach us something further about seeing, something similar and yet different: *What we do not see (with our physical eyes) may be the truth that is right in front of us.* Once upon a time, for example,

> A monk rode an ox into town and came to a group of people. The people asked him, "What are you looking for, monk?" He said, "I am looking for an ox." They all laughed. He rode his ox to the next group of people. They asked him, "What are you looking for, monk?" He said, "I am looking for an ox." They all laughed. He rode his ox to a third group of people. They asked him, "What are you looking for, monk?" He said, "I am looking for an ox." They said, "This is ridiculous. You are a man riding on an ox looking for an ox." The monk said, "So it is with you looking for God."[14]

I suspect this story needs no commentary.

Perhaps the classic Eurocentric story about seeing what is not there is Hans Christian Andersen's *The Emperor's New Clothes.* In this story two tricksters gain a plum assignment from the emperor of a fantasy kingdom with their claim to make clothing so beautiful and unique that only people who were unfit for their jobs or stupid could not see it. Well, no one wanted to appear stupid or unfit before her or his neighbors. So everyone pretended to "see" this new clothing on the emperor who was actually parading around in his BVDs. By perpetuating the deception, the people allowed themselves to be made fools, the tricksters to get away with the finest materials for themselves, and the emperor to be humiliated when a child announced what he simply saw: "He has nothing on." Because of their vanity and fearfulness, the people of this empire saw what they did not see and did not see what was right in front of their eyes.[15]

Well, guess what? Mark's story concurs! Consider the aforementioned episode involving the centurion. There the centurion perceives Jesus' special connection to God (15:39) even at the moment when God seems most absent to Jesus ("My God, my God, why have you forsaken me?" in 15:34). The Bartimaeus story may be read similarly. As Jesus encounters him, Jesus is steadfastly on his way to Jerusalem and the sure confrontation with the chief religious leaders that awaits him there. Nevertheless, when Bartimaeus has his sight restored, he immediately follows Jesus "on the way" to Jerusalem (10:52). Mark's telling of this story suggests Bartimaeus could see that this danger-filled way was indeed the "Way of the Lord." His sight caused him to join Jesus on this journey. Bartimaeus reminds me of Thornton's claim that seeing is the key discipline for the spiritual journey.

Here I will also mention a story in which the word *see* does not appear, but which, I think, shows us much about insightfulness. In Mark 14:3–9 a woman anoints Jesus' head–a ritual act performed on priests, kings, messiahs. But she does so to prepare for his burial. Her act suggests she *sees* both his summons and anointing by God for a special task in the world, and that he will die because of it. At this point in Mark's story, she is the only character to see clearly that both of these realities are true (compare her to Peter in 8:32).

In this second group of stories, Mark indicates that insightful people see what is not apparent to most folks. They see that a call from God and suffering because of that call may necessarily fit together. They see that the Way of the Lord leads into–not away from–confrontation with evil. They see that God is present even in moments when God seems most absent. They see where and how and when God is at work in the world even when surface appearances could suggest that God is not at work at all. Frankly, these seers may look like fools to most folks. But they are the ones who are not blinded by what they do not see. Thus, developing "the capacity for seeing the unseen" as the key discipline for the spiritual journey is affirmed again. In Mark's story those who see that God is present and at work in Jesus are the ones who follow him on the Way.

Summary: Mark's Call to See

Unlearning a lifetime of habitually seeing appearances is often difficult, but spiritual journeys require us to renew our power of vision.[16] So Mark's journey story shows us that following Jesus *on the way* calls forth an insightfulness that looks beneath the surface of any situation or circumstance for the truth hovering there. Insightful people take neither institutions nor individuals at "face value." They see beyond particular moments to the further implications, consequences, and possibilities of one's words and deeds. In addition, their sight is not limited by what they cannot see with their physical eyes. Instead, they are able to imagine, and thus *see*, what yet might be. According to Mark, followers of Jesus must be so insightful that they are not deceived by dark circumstances that scare them with suggestions of God's absence nor by pleasant appearances that actually mask the presence of evil.

Furthermore, this theme is so often present in so many *good* stories that the kind of sight or insightfulness we find in Mark is affirmed as characteristic of those who are authentically human. The stories also clarify the insightfulness for which Mark calls. They underscore Mark's story of authentic, insightful people as the ones who are not deceived by frogs or Claude Frollo or a beautiful temple façade before which scribes make long prayers as they pretend to be spiritual. They see the naked emperor. They see the yeast. They see themselves. They see that God is present and at work in Jesus as he travels the Way of the Lord. So they follow him on the Way, even to Jerusalem and what awaits him there.

Insightfulness for Twenty-First–Century People

If Mark is correct that insightfulness is characteristic of those who are authentically human, then it should be relevant for twenty-first–century North Americans no less than for the first-century people to whom Mark wrote. Let's consider this possibility.

Relevance in Our Culture

I often hear contemporary Western culture described in two ways. The first is as a "style over substance" culture that declares that we are what we look like. It seems to me that this description is used with good reason. We continue to be plagued by racism and sexism, age-old discrimination based on persons' external characteristics. In addition we suffer today from what psychologist Mary Pipher calls "lookism, which is the evaluation of a person solely on the basis of appearance," that is, having the right body, the right hair, the right clothes.[17]

A second description I often hear is that ours is a culture of consumption that declares that we are what we have. In a myriad of ways we are told that products can satisfy our longings and that happiness can be purchased in these "United States of Advertising."[18] Hebrew Bible scholar Clinton McCann has pointed out that a culture that promotes "getting all you can, canning all you get, and sitting on your can" necessarily leads people to ego-centeredness. But since practically no one applauds ego-centeredness, McCann claimed it has been renamed "autonomy," which is promoted today as an American virtue.[19]

So we are bombarded by images and messages that tell us that looking beautiful and appearing rich and successful in our houses, cars, clothes, boats, and so forth is the way to be happy. For our purposes, let us note how these perspectives call us in our evaluations of ourselves and of others to pay attention only to what we see with our physical eyes.

Is such a culture really so problematic? Mark's story with its call to us to be insightful people would answer with an emphatic Yes! Other *good* stories echo that yes. The truth about life and people usually rests beneath the surface and beyond any given moment. See what lies there, these stories insist, if you wish to live authentically. Today, many observers of our culture are showing us how true the stories are. They believe that the American obsession with appearances and consumption is indeed problematic. Consider, for example, how the emphasis on appearance is especially damaging for American adolescent girls. They learn that beauty is the defining characteristic for American women and obsess about clothes, make-up, and hair, but mostly about weight. On any given day in America half our teenage girls are dieting. One in five has an eating disorder. Pipher reports, "In all the years I've been a therapist, I've yet to meet one girl who likes her body....When I speak to classes, I ask any woman in the audience who feels good about her body to come forward...I have yet to have a woman come up."[20]

Our consumption is also causing a lot of misery. I won't belabor this point here. Probably most of us have heard that the objectification and commodification of nature is destroying this Earth that is God's gift to us. Probably most of us have heard that the rich are getting richer and the poor poorer. So I will simply reinforce the point by noting that disparities between rich and poor have doubled since

1962 so that in our time the wealthiest 20 percent of the world's population receives 83 percent of the world's income while the poorest 20 percent receives only 2 percent. Not only does this mean that people in the debt-ridden Two Thirds World are condemned to near hopeless poverty but in our country "trickle down" economics has also meant plant closings, the demise of mom-and-pop stores, the family farm crisis, and so on. People are displaced, anxious, find themselves in debt personally, and no longer believe in a better future for their kids.[21]

But remarkably, our consumption is problematic even for those of us who supposedly benefit from a consumer economy. Psychological researchers Richard Ryan and Tim Kasser have found that people for whom affluence is a priority are more depressed and anxious than others, report more behavioral problems, and score lower on measures of vitality and self-actualization. They call this "the dark side of the American dream."[22] Writer John Cheever has said that the main emotion of the adult in Northeastern America who has had all the advantages of wealth, education, and culture is disappointment.[23] Dorothee Soelle complains that our consumer culture has reduced all human needs into one universal need for money so that a main message we get from the media is that only success measured in dollars matters. Consequently, she says, people grow up without any education for joy.[24] Mary Pipher believes, "We wake in the night sorry for ourselves and our planet."[25]

Yet so many continue not to see this misery! The promotion of appearance and consumption are so ever present that many of us believe that political claims, advertising slogans, soap opera scripts, and "independent surveys" are telling the truth.[26] Spiritual teacher Parker Palmer laments these "illusions" in which we have invested so much of ourselves. We have personal illusions about our motives, abilities, and desires. We have societal illusions about what makes for success and happiness.[27] Such illusions have produced a "mass cultural trance," in the words of priest and spiritual director Richard Rohr. Consequently, we are in danger of sleepwalking through our lives. Significantly, Rohr also notes that this "trance" is not new to us now. The particular means of the trance (appearance and consumption) may be new, but not the trance itself. Societies have always encouraged sleepwalking so that we will stay in our appointed places rather than look around and say, "Something is wrong here!" Rohr claims that "all religious teachers have said this. We human beings do not naturally see. We have to be taught how to see. That's what religion is for."[28] And that's what Mark is doing! So, these commentaries on our culture and on our lives suggest to me that Mark's call to insightfulness is not merely relevant. It is urgently needed.

Relevance for the Church

We can also observe how particularly appropriate and relevant this call to see is for those of us who are Christian, and not just because it comes from one of our sacred texts. Though perhaps most Christians would enthusiastically agree with the cultural critique just offered, we in the church have not always withstood the seductions of consumption or the valuing of style over substance. My experience suggests, for example, that when Christians claim their church is growing, most of them are measuring growth in terms of numbers of people present rather than the faithfulness of their discipleship. Indeed, many of us have heard the semi-joke about how to measure the success of a pastor: by the three "B's", building, budgets, and baptisms. Activist and writer Ched Myers calls this the "edifice complex." The three "B's" and the number of people present are, of course, visible to anyone's physical eyes, while faithfulness is not. Churches with "more and bigger" appear successful. Many Christians seem satisfied with that appearance. Mark would not be.

There is also a second way Mark's call to see is particularly relevant to Christians. We have a history, it seems fair to say, of taking Paul's admonition to "walk by faith, not by sight" as justification for glorifying a "blind faith" that enables Christians readily to follow charismatic, smooth-talking, Bible-quoting, right-looking persons regardless of the fruits of their lives and especially if they are saying something we like hearing anyway. How else to explain Christians' support of the Crusades, the Inquisitions, the witch trials, even Hitler? How else to explain Christians' defense of slavery, segregation, and apartheid? How else to explain what has been happening for years in Northern Ireland between Protestants and Catholics? How else to explain Christians' endorsement of Jim Bakker and the PTL Club and other expressions of the "healthy, wealthy, and wise" gospel? How else to explain the oppression and abuse of women within the church—just how long might this list be? So often evil has abounded while we Christians have blindly been its staunchest supporters!

Paul's words, however, were not intended to evoke blind faith! In 2 Corinthians 4:1–5:10 Paul wrote about the ministry God had given him to do (4:1–6), which resulted in persecution, even to the point of death (4:7–12; see also 1:8–9). He continued his ministry, despite the threat of death, because of his hope of sharing in the life of God beyond this life (4:14; 5:1). His opponents could kill him, but he believed they could not take *life* from him. But he could not prove the existence of this life in God beyond death. Instead, he believed in the "eternal things which are not seen" (4:18). In this context, therefore, he declared that Christians "walk by faith, not by sight" (5:7). Paul was interested in Christians' not needing to see something with their physical eyes to believe that it was true.

Thus, Paul was much like Mark's centurion and Bartimaeus, who grasped that what they did *not* see was the truth right in front of their eyes. He never called believers to a blind faith that did not examine carefully and see clearly what was present. Indeed, in another part of the Corinthian correspondence, we find him afraid that the Corinthians were listening to those whom he referred to as "false apostles, deceitful workers, disguising themselves as apostles of Christ as Satan disguises himself as an angel of light" (2 Cor. 11:13–14). In this situation Paul called the Corinthians to "see the things in front of your face" (2 Cor. 10:7) and turn from the different gospel these people preached (2 Cor. 11:4). Rather than supporting blind faith, Paul joins Mark in advocating insightfulness for Christians who wish to live authentically before God.

For all the reasons just cited, and there are probably others, I believe that Mark's call to see is as relevant and timely today for North Americans generally and North American Christians specifically as it was for persons in the first-century world. Across the years one of our sacred stories reminds us of what it means to live authentically as the human beings God created us to be: We must be people who see if we would journey to God.

Concluding Thoughts

As we end this chapter, let us return for a moment to a story mentioned in the last chapter, Dante's *The Divine Comedy*. As Dante is journeying on his way, he is asked several times what he is doing in that place, since he is not yet dead. Sometimes he avoids the question, answering instead with comments about the area of Italy from which he has come. Sometimes he points to his guide as the reason he is there. But when he is asked again as he comes near the end of Purgatory and is close to passing over into Paradise, he answers, "I am traveling up through here *in order to be blind no longer*."[29]

Clearly the writer of the second gospel hoped those reading the story of Jesus' sacred journey would "be blind no longer." "See what you hear," Mark's Jesus exhorted his followers in the story. "See the yeast!" "See yourselves!" "Do not be deceived!" Mark's story shows that evil will absolutely try to lead astray even God's own, so we must see! False prophets may do signs and wonders or make wonderful-sounding declarations in the name of God. That guy dying up there does not look like God's son, but is. God may seem absent, but is not. The temple may appear beautiful even while it houses a den of robbers. To be authentically human, as God intended that we be, to follow Jesus on the Way, we must see. Mark tells us this over and over again in the story.

"See!" many *good* stories urge us, adding their own calls to insightfulness and affirming Mark's call to us. "See!" they implore us, for Claude Frollo is the monster, the emperor has no clothes on, and the first key to wisdom is to realize that all that we see is not what it seems. We need today to be insightful, for despite what our culture tells us, happiness cannot be bought, and a person's appearance is no way to judge her or his humanity. We Christians should not affirm a blind faith, but should seek instead the deeply perceptive and insightful faith that Mark's story advocates.

"See!" we are told, for the truth about people and circumstances usually lies behind the appearances and beyond the moment. If the surfaces and externals are all we can see, we might one day kiss a handsome prince or princess only to discover he or she is really a frog.

CHAPTER 3

"What Do You Wish That I Would Do for You?"

(Mark 10:51)

ONCE UPON A TIME a medieval Irish monk died and was buried, as was the custom, in the monastery wall. One day the monks heard noises from within the wall and removed the stones to find their brother alive and well. He began to tell them what he had learned on his journey beyond. And everything he said was contrary to the teachings of the church. So the brothers put him back in the wall and sealed the crypt forever.[1]

ONCE UPON A TIME a blind beggar named Bartimaeus cried out to Jesus for mercy as Jesus and the crowd surrounding him passed near Bartimaeus on the way to Jerusalem. Though the crowd tried to silence him, he persisted in his calls for mercy. Jesus heard him and told the people, "Bring the brother to me." Then Jesus asked him, "What do you wish that I would do for you?" Bartimaeus responded, "Rabbi, let me *see*." Jesus granted his request. Immediately Bartimaeus *saw*. When he saw, he followed Jesus on the way (to Jerusalem and the cross).

Mark 10:46–52, PARAPHRASED

As enjoyable as Mark's miracle story is, it should hardly be taken to indicate that this gospel writer viewed Jesus as a genie from a magic lamp granting whatever wishes were requested from him. In fact, in the story that immediately precedes this one in Mark, Jesus posed to James and John (10:36) the same question he asked of Bartimaeus: "What do you wish that I would do for you?" But Jesus did not grant them what they sought. Despite Jesus' plain teaching about the suffering that awaited him in Jerusalem, James and John asked to sit on his right and left hands when he came into his glory. There is, of course, all the difference in the world between their request and that of Bartimaeus. Even when Bartimaeus was blind, he could see better than they.

We noted in the previous chapter how seeing is the key discipline for the spiritual journey. We also noted its significance to the writer of the second gospel. In this chapter we take a further step on this way. We will explore those in Mark's gospel who see and those who do not and why, and what impact a person's sight or lack thereof has on what happens in the story and on us as readers of this story.

Literary critics often divide the characters in Mark's story into three groups: the twelve chosen disciples, the religious leaders, and the so-called minor characters. We will first examine each of these groups in terms of their sight. Then we will check the narrative for hints as to why some see and some do not. We may well be a bit unsettled by the results of this study, for we will find that the most unexpected people are the ones who see and follow the way of the Lord in Mark's story. We will then note how persistent such a theme is in other *good* stories. Thus, other stories again help us see more clearly Mark's portrayal of the human condition. Finally, we can confirm here as well that this 2,000-year-old Markan portrait of authentic humanness is uncannily accurate by showing its relevance for today, especially for those of us who would be considered among the most religious folk of our time.

Those Who Do Not See

The role of the twelve disciples in Mark, along with Mark's view of discipleship, is a major issue in contemporary Markan studies. Since at least the early sixties,[2] the Twelve's lack of sight has been a virtual truism among Mark scholars. We can do more than merely declare that they are blind, however. We can review the relevant texts in order to characterize their blindness, especially in light of Mark's call to see, as described earlier.

A brief comment is in order about "finding" the Twelve in Mark's story. I am convinced that Mark's references to "disciples" in the story indicate a large group of followers of Jesus that includes the Twelve but is not limited to them. For example, 4:10 refers to "those around him with the Twelve." Verses 15:40–41 tell us about women who followed him from the days in Galilee. We are also told that people such as Levi and Bartimaeus followed Jesus, but they are not named as members of the Twelve. When we read about "the disciples," therefore, we can assume the Twelve are included but are not alone. At key moments in the story, however, they are singled out. So I will talk about the disciples generally, but I will focus on the Twelve because specific instances of blindness are so often focused on them.

We noted in the last chapter that in their discussion with Jesus in 8:14–16, the disciples could not see beyond that which was literal and concrete. Remember when Jesus warned them about the "yeast" of the Pharisees and Herod? Despite having twice seen him feed multitudes with miniscule amounts of bread, the disciples feared that he meant their one loaf of bread was insufficient. They demonstrate this kind of blindness several times in Mark's gospel. A hemorrhaging woman touches the hem of Jesus' garment and is healed. Jesus, aware that power has gone out from him, turns and asks, "Who touched my clothes?" The disciples see only the crowds jostling and bumping into Jesus and are incredulous at his question: "You see this crowd pressing around you and you say, 'Who touched me?'" (5:31). They cannot see the possibility that someone in the crowd might touch Jesus with purpose or that Jesus could be aware of that purpose.

A comparable moment occurs in chapter 6, the first of Mark's remarkable feeding stories. When the crowds follow Jesus and company into the wilderness, and Jesus tells the disciples to feed the multitude, the disciples see only too many people and too little bread. Jesus, however, sees the great crowd like sheep without a shepherd. He has compassion on them, teaches them despite his fatigue, and feeds them fully, even with the scant amount of bread available (6:31–37). Similarly, in 13:1 one of the disciples exclaims over the temple façade. Earlier, however, Jesus had cursed the temple (11:15–17), warned them of the scribes there who only appeared religious (12:38–40), and called their attention to the widow who had had her "whole life" taken from her by the corrupt economics practiced in the temple (12:41–44). Despite Jesus' cautions, however, the disciples are impressed by the surface greatness of the temple buildings.

Given these failures, are we surprised that the disciples struggled to see Jesus' intent for his parables (cf. 4:13; 7:17–18)? I think not! Furthermore, we should now be prepared for their blindness to larger matters, such as the grand news that Jesus brought, his proclamation that the *basileia* of God has drawn near. So in 9:34 we find them arguing among themselves about who is the greatest. Jesus responds by putting a child in the midst of the Twelve and telling them that whoever receives such a child in his name receives God (9:36–37). Nevertheless, shortly thereafter they rebuke those who bring children to Jesus (10:13). In the first-century Mediterranean world children were among the "least of these," an insignificant part of an adult-oriented culture with no honor for themselves.[3] The disciples treated them accordingly. Jesus, however, received and blessed children as members of God's *basileia,* where all are welcomed and no one is first or last or least (10:14–16). His attitude toward these "least ones" is a clear sign of the transformation of relationships among people that Jesus proclaimed in God's name.

But the Twelve did not see that the *basileia* of God gives birth to this radical new order among people. Consequently, they did not see the threat Jesus posed to the old order. So Peter responded to Jesus' first announcement that he was going to die by rebuking Jesus for saying so (and got rebuked himself in return! 8:32–33). James and John followed Jesus' last, most detailed prediction of his death (10:33–34) by asking him to let them sit at his right and left hands when he came into his glory (10:37), as we noted earlier. When James's and John's request created a "situation" among the Twelve (10:41), Jesus responded by reiterating both his vision ("whoever wishes to become great among you is to be a servant of you all, and whoever wishes to be first among you is to be a slave of all," 10:43–44) and its cost ("the New Human Being/Son of Man[4] came…to give his life as a ransom for many," 10:45). Despite Jesus' efforts to teach them, as the religious leaders closed in on him, Judas betrayed him, Peter denied him, and the rest fled Gethsemane in fear.

Clearly the Twelve in Mark see what is literally in front of their (physical) eyes. They see only an actual loaf of bread, too many people and too little food, a sower sowing seed, an insignificant child, the temple facade, the political-economic-religious system with its hierarchical relationships among people as it had always operated in their world. They are easily swayed by surface appearances and lack the kind of insight for which Mark calls. So of course they do not see people as Jesus saw them or see that the *basileia* of God has drawn near. They are blind to the implications of Jesus' words. They are blind to the possibility of transformative ways of relating to God and one another in the "discipleship of equals" (to use feminist scholar Elisabeth Schüssler Fiorenza's term). Such a community is characterized by practices of inclusiveness, justice, and service. In such a community individuals are freed from whatever binds them. Because the disciples cannot envision such a community, they cannot see the threat God's *basileia* poses to those invested in the old order. Nor can they see that God can bring redemption out of unjust suffering on behalf of this vision. We might reasonably conclude that they are blind to what God wills or what God is doing in their world despite all they have seen in their days of following Jesus.

Those Who See

The other two character groups, the minor characters and the religious leaders, fall into the category of those who see. Many readers of Mark will be surprised to find the religious leaders showing up here. After examining the minor characters I will show why I believe they belong in this category.

The Minor Characters

Another truism of Markan studies is the positive portrayal of many of the minor characters who appear in the story. Certain of these folk can be treated, according to the methods of literary critics, as a single character. They share similar traits and a continuing role in the plot of the story in relationship to one another.[5] These characters, including the leper who asked for cleansing, the paralytic who came through the roof and his friends, Jairus the synagogue ruler, the hemorrhaging woman, the Syrophoenician woman, the demon-possessed boy's father who cried out, "I believe, help my unbelief," Bartimaeus, the widow with the two coins, the anointing woman, and the centurion at the cross create some of the most memorable moments in Mark's story.

Scholars have noted two traits these characters have in common. One is their persistent faith in Jesus, which enables many of them to overcome obstacles to encountering him. A second common trait is that they show what it means to serve others. These two traits make them perfect literary "foils" for the Twelve, who know little about persistent faith and virtually nothing about service.[6]

We are interested, however, in the way members of this character group exhibit the ability to *see* as Mark calls us to do. Bartimaeus is clearly the perfect example of one with such insight. Given the opportunity to request something of Jesus, Bartimaeus asked to see. With his sight restored, he immediately followed Jesus on the way to Jerusalem and the cross (10:46–52). The centurion also, as discussed in the previous chapter, displayed significant insight when he saw a connection between the way Jesus died and Jesus' being the son of God (15:39). Another example is the story of the scribe who heard Jesus' disputes with the religious leaders in the temple and *saw* that Jesus answered them well (12:28). Then he showed understanding of Jesus' declaration of the two greatest commandments, saying that these are "much greater than all whole burnt offerings and sacrifices" (12:32–33). At this point Mark notes that Jesus *saw* that the scribe himself had answered wisely (12:34).

Although "seeing" language is not specifically used in other stories involving minor characters, many of these episodes nonetheless show these characters to be insightful, as Mark wished people to be. For example: A leper approached Jesus, though cultural rules said he must not, and said to him, "If you will, you are able to cleanse me" (1:40). Thus, he gives a strong affirmation of Jesus' power and compassion that is all the more extraordinary for how early in Jesus' ministry it occurs, according to Mark. Similarly, the hemorrhaging woman, working her way through a crowd where she is not welcomed because of her uncleanness, reasoned, "If I touch even his clothes, I will be saved" (5:28).

Then there is the Syrophoenician woman, who is the only person in Mark's gospel to address Jesus as "Lord." Remarkably, she does so even as Jesus initially refuses her request to heal her daughter because of her ethnicity. She is also the only person in the gospel to best Jesus in an argument when she insists that even the dogs under the table are allowed to eat the children's crumbs. With these words she persuades him to change his mind about her request (7:24–30).[7] We might claim that she *sees* the inclusiveness of Jesus' mission more clearly than even he does at this point in Mark's story. Finally, we can note that the anointing woman in 14:3–9 is the only person in the gospel who *sees,* prior to the cross, what Jesus' destiny must be.

These characters, therefore, are not only foils for the Twelve in terms of faith and service. They also *see* how God is at work in Jesus. Considering the barriers many of them crossed to get to Jesus, we may fairly conclude that they saw their inclusion in the *basileia* of God that he proclaimed and were determined to receive their place. Moreover, at least some of them saw what his destiny must be for practicing such inclusiveness and justice, but they followed him still. Their perception and insight contrast sharply with the blindness of the Twelve. They exemplify the sight for which Mark's story, along with other good stories, calls.

The Religious Leaders

The religious leaders in Mark may also be treated as a single character because of their similar traits and their collective and ongoing role in the story's plot. All of them are in positions of authority and leadership in the Israel of Jesus' day. All of them are opposed to Jesus from the beginning of the story. Scholars usually classify them as blind along with the Twelve.[8] But I believe Mark's story is more complex than that. I believe, in at least one sense, that they can see quite well. Let's consider the following texts.

When Jesus announced forgiveness of the paralytic's sins in 2:5, the scribes grasped the implications of his words immediately. They questioned in their hearts, "Who is able to forgive sins except God alone?" (2:6). When Jesus entered a synagogue where there was a man with a withered hand, the Pharisees watched him to see whether or not he would heal the man on the sabbath (3:1–2). They do not wonder *if* Jesus can heal him. At this point in Mark's story they had seen his power clearly. Further, in this episode Jesus challenged them, "Is it lawful on the sabbath to do good or to do evil, to save life or to kill?" (3:4). When they could not answer his challenge without betraying their hardened hearts, they left the synagogue and immediately plotted with the Herodians to kill him (3:6). Their plot suggests that even this early in the narrative they saw the threat he was to the religious system of the day, a system that served them well. Similarly, after he cursed the temple for having become a den of robbers (11:15–17), the chief religious leaders sought a way to kill him (11:18). Their scheming suggests they also clearly saw how he jeopardized the political-economic-religious system that they operated with the temple as its centerpiece.

But the key text for arguing that the religious leaders were not blind is Jesus' parable of the workers in the vineyard in 12:1–11. In that parable the workers choose to kill the owner's son precisely because they recognize that he is the son, not because they do not know what they are doing (12:7–8). Then, as if to underscore the point that the religious leaders are not blind, Mark concludes this episode by relating how they wanted to arrest Jesus on the spot because they understood that he told this parable against them (12:12).

If we apply our definition of sight (the ability to see beneath surface appearances and beyond any given moment to consequences, implications, possibilities, etc.) to the religious leaders, we must conclude that they could see quite well. Whereas the Twelve were blind to Jesus' vision of the *basileia* of God, which transforms the way the people of God relate to one another and to God, the religious leaders "got it" clearly and early in the story. They indeed saw the transformation that Jesus wanted to bring about.

And yet the contrast between what happens as a result of their sight and what happens as a result of the sight of the minor characters is as great as the contrast between the sight of the minor characters and the blindness of the Twelve. What is going on here?

Sight and Blindness, Reception and Rejection in Mark

Are there hints in the narrative as to why the Twelve are blind, the minor characters see and follow Jesus on the Way, and the religious leaders see but reject Jesus and the Way he journeyed? The insights of liberationist biblical scholars applied to Mark's story are revealing for us.

Attending to Power Dynamics

Liberationists insist that we name and attend to the power dynamics in any situation we encounter, including those involving biblical texts. New Testament scholar Sharon Ringe, for example, has argued that the parable of the unforgiving servant in Matthew 18:21–35 can become a death sentence if the unjust power relationships in the context into which the parable may be read are not considered. This parable portrays God's unmerited and unlimited forgiveness and calls God's people to do likewise. But a woman in an abusive relationship may be convinced by the parable that if God can forgive so unworthy a creature, she must in turn forgive any wrongs done to her. So she forgives her abuser and returns home again and again even though the injustice on his side of the relationship isn't addressed. And sometimes she dies at his hands.[9]

While Ringe's article specifically addresses the power dynamics in which biblical texts are read, her concerns about unjust power relationships are more broadly applicable. Since these relationships have such enormous consequences for the people involved, we should be attentive to them wherever we find them, including within the biblical texts themselves. Therefore, in light of the challenges of Ringe and other liberationists, let's check the power relationships being played out on the pages of Mark's story.

Elisabeth Schüssler Fiorenza offers an analysis of the global social order in terms of a "kyriarchal pyramid" that will help us. By using her new word *kyriarchy* (meaning "rule of the lord") instead of patriarchy, she clarifies that not all men rule over all women. Instead, the rule of the emperor/master/lord/father/husband over his subordinates creates a complex social pyramid of graduated dominations and subordinations in the world.

Such a pyramid is not only in place today but was also true of the ancient world.[10] Thus, the religious authorities in Mark would have occupied or been near the positions of power and privilege at the top of first-century Israelite society, where religion, politics, and economics coexisted. Most of the minor characters would have been on the bottom of such a pyramid. Indeed, a leper, a Syrophoenician woman, a blind beggar, and a widow might best be imagined as beneath that pyramid! Not only were they politically powerless and economically exploited, but the religion of the day compounded their marginalization by declaring them unclean. Finally, the Twelve, most of whom were lowly peasants, would be placed near the bottom, but apparently still on, a first-century kyriarchal pyramid.[11]

Before going further, we should remember the impact of Jesus' mission in Mark. Both his proclamation ("if anyone wishes to be first, that one must be last of all and servant of all," etc.) and his practice (touching a leper, calling a tax collector, having women disciples, receiving children, etc.) would undermine such a societal structure. Kyriarchal pyramids were exactly the old order he sought to transform into the discipleship of equals in the *basileia* of God.

The Religious Leaders' Allegiance to Power

Since the religious leaders reside at the pinnacle of the pyramid of their day, they have "everything to lose" should Jesus' mission succeed *if* their primary allegiance is to their position, power, and privilege. As Mark's narrative unfolds, that appears to be exactly where their allegiance lies. A telling text is 11:27–33. The religious leaders ask Jesus the source of his authority to disrupt the temple commerce (which he had done in 11:15–16). He responds by asking them from whence John the Baptist's authority came: from God or from humans. They caucus among themselves, discussing the rock and hard place between which Jesus has put them. If they say John's authority was from heaven, Jesus will want to know why they did not believe him. But if they say it came from humans, they will face the crowd's ire, for the people view John as a true prophet. Notice what is not part of their discussion: the truth. They never ask themselves, "Where did John's authority come from? Might God have sent him?" They do not reckon with that question or its implications. They are only interested in saving their honor, positions, and power.

Indeed, the religious leaders in Mark would not have opened themselves to such a question. The religious-political-economic system they controlled was centered in the temple. In addition, the temple symbolized the presence of God among God's people. Given these two realities, we may not be out of bounds if we conclude that the religious leaders in Mark's story had equated their system with God. They had fully invested themselves in serving this God through their religion, politics, and economics. No doubt they loved their God, for this God served them well, granting them privileges, making them powerful. Borrowing words from twelfth-century spiritual teacher Bernard of Clairvaux, we might say they loved God for self's sake.[12] Since Jesus, and John before him, threatened the temple system, the religious leaders could not consider the prospect that God was the source of the troublemakers' authority. Such a consideration would require them to allow the possibility that God was separate from their system. What upheaval for them and their way of viewing the world if that should be true!

So there is no coincidence that we first hear of the chief priests' joining the death plot against Jesus just after he cursed the temple (11:18) or that the main charge on which they sought Jesus' death sentence was that he said he would destroy the temple (14:57–58).[13] Though Mark's Jesus never actually said those words, his mission would indeed destroy the temple as the religious leaders knew it. This they saw clearly. They were not blind to what Jesus was about.

Of course, from Mark's perspective, their sight is quite limited. Their investment in their religious-political-economic system does not allow them to be open to God should God act apart from this system. Indeed, their vision does not allow them to see God as Mark believed God to be, as One who receives whoever needs God, including those outside the "boundaries" (such as lepers, tax collectors, widows, Gentiles, children, etc.); as One who is not constrained even by centuries of religious practice if those practices produce only the "right kind of people" rather than pure hearts (7:1–23); as One who is no longer encountered in a temple that has become a den of robbers.[14] Using language from the previous chapter, we can say that Mark believed the religious leaders were caught off guard by God's eschatological activity in the world. They cannot see God as Mark does.

The Minor Characters' Lack of Allegiance to Power

But the minor characters can and do see God thusly. As mentioned, most of them should probably be imagined as underneath a kyriarchal pyramid. While the religious leaders had everything to lose should Jesus succeed, this group had nothing to lose in terms of power, privilege, or status. Thus, we should not expect to find them invested in maintaining the religious-political-economic system of their time, and we do not. Note, for example, how they ignore the cultural rules designed to keep people like themselves in "their place." A leper and a Syrophoenician woman, both extremely unclean in first-century Jewish society, draw near to Jesus with requests. An unclean hemorrhaging woman wades through a crowd to touch him. Bartimaeus shouts his desire for mercy from Jesus even when he has been told to shush. A woman crashes a dinner party to which she apparently was not invited to anoint him for burial. Owing no allegiance to the way things were in their world evidently freed them to *see* Jesus' message about God's eschatological work in the world. They could see that God was ushering in God's *basileia*, which meant the transformation of their relationships to God and one another. It also made them receptive to Jesus' offer of God's radical new order—with great energy and enthusiasm they claimed their places in God's *basileia* and followed Jesus on his way.

The Twelve's Hopes for Power

What then of the Twelve? One of the remarkable things about the Twelve in Mark's story is that at times they are so faithful. When Jesus called, they followed immediately (note 1:16–20), leaving everything behind (10:28). They journey with Jesus. They successfully join in his mission, preaching repentance, casting out demons, and healing the sick (6:7–13). And yet they are blind. Whereas both the religious leaders and the minor characters see that Jesus envisions an order for God's people other than a kyriarchal pyramid, the Twelve do not see any possibility other than such a pyramid. To use a contemporary phrase, they never "think outside the box."

A revealing text regarding them is 10:23–26. Jesus has just encountered the rich man who would not give up his possessions to join Jesus (10:17–22). Afterward, Jesus comments to his disciples, "How hard for the ones having riches to enter the *basileia* of God!" (10:23). By now followers of Mark's Jesus in the story (not to mention readers of Mark's story) should understand why this is hard. Jesus wishes to undo the societal structures and practices that put people in positions of wealth, privilege, and power over others. The disciples, however, do not see at all. First they are amazed at Jesus' comment (10:24). Then, when he repeats himself, they are astonished and respond, "Who is able to be saved?" (10:26). They sound as though they consider riches to reflect God's blessing and approval. They clearly don't see what Jesus has told them.

A critical question now is this: Are the Twelve unable or unwilling to see? At first glance the answer may seem elementary. If they were unable to see, what would be the point of Jesus' trying to get them to see? But perhaps surprisingly, I believe Mark's answer is that they are both. In Mark 4:24–25 Jesus says to them, "See what you hear! By which measure you measure it will be measured to you and added to you. For to those who have, more will be given, and to those who have not, even what they have will be taken from them." Jesus' words indicate that those who respond to Jesus' call to "see what you hear" will see more and more. Those who are unwilling to respond, however, will become unable to see anything. So, as the Twelve apparently choose only to see their world as it has always been, they become unable to see what God is doing through Jesus.

If the source of the Twelve's blindness to Jesus in Mark is their unwillingness and consequent inability to see anything other than the world as it is, then we can understand several of their interactions with Jesus more clearly. Their attitude seems to be that if such a pyramid-like structure is inevitably in place in the world, one's goal should be to get to the top of it. So they argue with one another over who is the greatest (9:34). They forbid others to cast out demons in Jesus' name because those persons are not part of their group (9:38). They try to keep children from Jesus (10:13). James and John ask to sit at Jesus' right and left hands in his glory (10:37). Furthermore, I suspect we do not go too far if we understand them as hoping to use the power of God at work in Jesus to get themselves to the top in their world. Why else focus on Jesus' glory, limit access to Jesus to themselves, and be concerned for who is the greatest among them?

Indeed, the reason for their unwillingness to see in the first place appears to be that they had not given up their hopes of becoming "kings of the hill." Perhaps not terribly unlike the religious leaders, the real allegiance of the Twelve rested in their own positions of power, that is, in themselves. It appears that they too sought a God who would serve them well and help them get what they desired. They too appear to love God for self's sake. They had not denied themselves at all. Since the religious leaders wanted to maintain their power, they saw the threat Jesus posed to them. Because the Twelve wanted to gain power, they refused to see that Jesus taught another way, one that would transform power structures that dominated and subordinated into the discipleship of equals. As they refused to see, they became blind.

Lessons from the Power Dynamics

Following the lead of liberationists so that we have paid attention to the power dynamics in the world of this text leads to a significant conclusion. We discover that allegiance to power and self (and to a God who will serve self well) versus allegiance to God affects one's ability to see and receive what one sees. The more the people in Mark's story were invested in getting themselves to the top or in staying at the top of the power structures of the day, the more blind they were to the presence of God outside those structures. Or if they saw work that would transform those structures, they rejected that work as God's work.

The flip side, of course, is that the more the people in Mark's story were not invested in getting to the top of the power structures of the day, the more they saw and received what God was doing in the world. Liberation theologians and biblical scholars have long observed the "hermeneutical advantage of the poor." What they mean by this term is that marginalized people have an easier time seeing Jesus' message of the transforming power of God's *basileia*. Perhaps this review of Mark's story helps us understand why they speak about this advantage. Doubtless, the poor are not inherently more insightful than others. Instead, as we can see from the minor characters in Mark's story, the reality of their lives is that they have little opportunity to "get to the top" of the power structures of their day or to gain wealth, privilege, and status. So they face fewer temptations to invest themselves in these kinds of ego-gratifications. Thus, they are freer to open themselves to God's transforming, eschatological activity in the world.

The religious leaders and the Twelve, on the other hand, belonged on the kyriarchal pyramid of their day. They had opportunities to advance their wealth, privilege, and power. In addition, they had more religious education and service–the religious leaders in the traditions of the elders, the Twelve as a result of being with Jesus. Consequently, they appear to be the ones best able to see where and how and when God was at work in the world. But precisely because of these advantages, they faced greater temptations to commit themselves to ego-gratification while calling it religious service. If they yielded to this temptation, then they would not be open to whatever God might be doing in their world.

All of this creates quite a challenge for the ones reading (and the one writing) a book such as this one, who are likely to be educated, middle-class (at least) Westerners with a history of religious involvement. The truth is, most of us have more in common with the Twelve and the religious leaders in Mark than with the minor characters. The truth is, Mark is asking some unsettling questions directly of us. But is Mark telling us that we are doomed to be blind to God or to reject the work of God if we see it creating upheaval for us personally?

Thankfully, the answer is no. Consider Mark 10:14–15. In these verses Mark records Jesus' announcing that the *basileia* of God belongs to children and that "whoever does not receive the *basileia* of God like a child will *not* enter it" (emphasis taken from the Greek text). Bible readers have typically understood Jesus' saying to mean that true disciples must be innocent, trusting, guileless, and so forth, as children are. But that interpretation is based on contemporary views of children. As we have noted, in the first-century Mediterranean world, children were among the "least of these," as were most of the minor characters in Mark's story. Thus, to receive God's *basileia* as children is to receive it like those who have "nothing to lose" in terms of the power structures of the day because they are not invested in gaining positions, privilege, and wealth for themselves.

Such people are free to pledge their allegiance wholly to God and open themselves to God's transforming eschatological activity in the world. We do not have to be marginalized people to enter God's *basileia,* as the scribe who understood the two greatest commandments (12:32–34) and the centurion at the cross (15:39) demonstrate. Both of them would have been near the top of a kyriarchal pyramid. Mark shows us we can choose to be like the minor characters in the story, who stand outside the power structures of the day, who see that things are not always what they appear to be, and who commit themselves to work with God however radical God's work may be. But let us acknowledge the cost of such choices, which Mark also shows us. Authentic self-denial is never easy. But Mark shows us it is the way we must journey if we desire to become the persons God created us to be.

Affirmation and Clarification from the Stories

So, following this review of who sees and who does not in Mark's story, we are able to see that in Mark the people who appear to be the most unlikely ones in that culture are the most insightful people. Those most politically and economically powerless, who were also considered most unclean and farthest from God, are exactly the ones who see where and how God is at work in their world and receive what God is doing. As we have done before, we can observe how frequently this theme is found in good stories.

Stories of Unlikely Seers

A number of these stories can be found in the Hebrew Scriptures. Would you have chosen a lying, conniving Jacob for anything, much less to be a key player in God's unfolding salvation of the world? Would you have thought the greatest story of love and devotion would be about a Moabite woman named Ruth? Would you have expected the harp-playing, slingshot-wielding, youngest son of a shepherd to become Israel's most celebrated king?

Jewish folklore continues this theme. We find in another of the Elijah stories involving Rabbi Joshua ben Levi that Rabbi Joshua asks Elijah when the Messiah will come. "Go and ask him yourself," replies Elijah. "Where is he?" asks the rabbi. "Sitting at the gates of the city," is Elijah's response. When the rabbi then asks how to recognize him, Elijah says, "He is sitting among the poor covered with wounds."[15]

Our Jewish sisters and brothers have no monopoly on such stories. The Islamic tradition treasures tales of Nasrudin the fool, who is usually the wisest person in the tales. In one story, for example, Nasrudin is eating his usual fare of chick peas, gruel, and stale bread. Meanwhile his neighbor feasts on food from the king's own table. His neighbor calls out to him, "What a pity! If only you would accommodate the king and tell him more of what he wants to hear, you'd dine on rich food and drink like I do." Nasrudin responds, "If only you'd learn to savor the taste of chick peas and gruel, then you would live in freedom from the king."[16]

In a Sufi story of Jesus, Jesus and an elder were talking of eternal things when a notorious robber saw them, longed to join them, and dared to fall into step beside them. When the elder saw the robber, he stepped closer to Jesus so as to shut the robber out. Meanwhile the robber was berating himself for thinking he could draw near to someone so holy and truthful. Then Jesus spoke to both of them, "From this moment on you are forgiven and all your past is gone, erased as though it never happened." To the robber he said, "Your evil deeds are forgotten because you were humble before us." To the elder he said, "And your good deeds are all gone because of your self-righteousness and disdain for your neighbor." With that the robber became Jesus' disciple, and the elder left him.[17]

Stories of Unlikely Blindness

The last story serves as a segue to what may be a further surprise in this study of Mark. The most religious people in Mark's story—those we would most expect to be working alongside Jesus—are the ones most problematic for his mission on behalf of God's *basileia*. One group creates problems because it will not see the new possibilities he offers. The other group is a thorn for Jesus because it sees but rejects the implications of his message. Again, we find that good stories tell this same story over and over.

Some of these *good* stories tell their tales with humor. They bring forth a wry chuckle and quiet "aha" from hearers, as does the story of the Irish monk with which this chapter began. Or as does the Russian folktale that storyteller William White calls "Three Holy Men." In this story a high-ranking religious leader hears of three men living on an island who devote themselves to prayer and worship. The religious leader decides he must check them out. He assumes that since they are under no one's supervision, they are probably doing things wrongly. So he has himself rowed out to their island where he observes their spiritual practices. Then he instructs them in the proper way to pray. In the boat on the way back to shore at the end of the day, he is congratulating himself for doing his duty well and enlightening those poor souls. But then he notices a light on the horizon. It gets ever brighter because it is approaching his boat. When it finally draws near enough, the religious leader sees that it is a torch held by one of the island men walking to him on the water so that he can ask about a portion of the prayer instruction he fears he has forgotten.[18]

Some of these *good* stories are particularly poignant, such as "The Tale of the Fugitive," in which a young man fleeing from soldiers took refuge in a village. The people there hid him and cared for him. But the soldiers found out where he was. They threatened to kill the villagers at dawn the next day unless they handed over the fugitive. The people asked their minister what to do. The minister withdrew to his room to read his Bible in search of an answer. Shortly before dawn his eyes fell on these words: "It is better that one man dies than that the whole people be lost." The minister told the soldiers where the man was hidden. They led him away to kill him. The people were relieved to have their problem solved. That night, however, the minister was visited by an angel who asked him, "What have you done? Don't you know that you have handed over the Messiah?" "How could I know?" the minister asked anxiously. The angel answered, "If, instead of reading your Bible, you had visited this young man just once and looked into his eyes, you would have known."[19]

Others of these *good* stories are neither humorous nor poignant. Their moods are darker, their tales troubling. In Nathaniel Hawthorne's *The Scarlet Letter*, the Rev. Arthur Dimmesdale urged Hester Prynne at the time of her public, Puritanical shaming to name the father of her child. If she did not, she would "tempt him–yea, compel him as it were–to add hypocrisy to sin."[20] In the end he was himself the man with whom she had committed adultery.

A story of the water of life begins with the great water wishing to make itself known to people. So it bubbled up in an artesian well where it flowed without effort or limit. People flocked to it and were nourished by it. Before too long, however, some persons fenced the well and claimed ownership of the property around it. They charged admission, put locks on the gates, and made elaborate laws regarding who could come to the well.

> Soon the well was the property of the powerful and the elite. The water was angry and offended; it stopped flowing and began to bubble up in another place. The people who owned the first well were so engrossed in their power systems and ownership that they did not notice the water had vanished. They continued selling the nonexistent water, and few people noticed that the true power was gone. But some dissatisfied people searched with great courage and found the new artesian well. Soon that well was under the control of the property owners, and the same fate overtook it. The spring took itself to yet another place.
>
> And on and on and on the story goes.[21]

One of the most disquieting of these stories is Dostoevsky's "The Grand Inquisitor." In the story Jesus returns to Earth for a short while during the Inquisition in sixteenth-century Spain to share mercy with the people. But the cardinal who heads the Inquisition orders his guards to arrest Jesus. His power is so great that the people stand back without protest. As Jesus is led away, all those in the crowd prostrate themselves before the Grand Inquisitor. The old man blesses them in silence and passes on. Later, visiting Jesus in the prison, the cardinal says to him,

> "You wanted to gain man's [sic] love so that he would follow You of his own free will, fascinated and captivated by You. In place of the clear and rigid ancient law, You made man decide about good and evil for himself, with no other guidance than Your example…There is nothing more alluring to man than freedom of conscience, but neither is there anything more agonizing…I tell You…that man has no more pressing, agonizing need than the need to find someone to whom he can hand over as quickly as possible the gift of freedom with which the poor wretch comes into the world…We have the right to preach to man that what matters is not freedom of choice or love, but a mystery that he must worship blindly, even at the expense of his conscience, and that is exactly what we have done. We have corrected Your work."[22]

Learning from Mark and the Stories

It seems to me that these many stories suggest that Mark understood well the part of the human condition that longs for the experience of God in our lives. Ruth, Rabbi Joshua, the three holy men, both thief and elder in the Sufi story, and even the Grand Inquisitor put themselves in positions where they might find God. In Mark's story the Twelve answered Jesus' call to follow, many of the minor characters overcame obstacles to get to him, and even the religious leaders were clearly students of the traditions of the elders that had been handed down to them. But the stories further and more hauntingly suggest that Mark also grasped one of the ragged edges of the human condition: the desire to experience God on our own terms, according to our self-interests and concerns.

So Mark and the stories insist that our religiousness is no guarantee of the insightfulness we need to travel the Way of the Lord. Our religious service may even be a stumbling block for ourselves and others. As a result of that service we may create systems and structures for doing the work of God that we then equate with God and come to love because this God serves us well! The more we have pledged ourselves to these expressions of self-centeredness (and worshiping a God who serves us well is an expression of self-centeredness), the more likely we are not to see the Spirit at work in unexpected people or places or circumstances, or if we see such work, to reject it even if it is the Spirit's work. The stories, including Mark's story, warn us that we then become like those who lock seers away in monastery walls forever. Or we believe we can and must correct God's work. Or we flee from Gethsemane when the soldiers come. Or we are the ones who turn the Messiah over to the soldiers. Or we crucify him ourselves, all the while passing ourselves off as the most religious of people, thus adding hypocrisy to our sin.

On the surface such people appear to have all the necessary advantages for seeing God. But those very advantages often become temptations to pursue ego-gratification disguised as service to God, as the elder in the Sufi story, the well owners in the living water story, the Grand Inquisitor, the Twelve, and Mark's religious leaders demonstrate. Church historian Penrose St. Amant once declared that when religion goes bad, it becomes demonic. The stories demonstrate that demonic is not too strong a word for describing what happens when religious people want God's presence only according to their self-interests.

Thus, Mark and the stories affirm a second significant conclusion of our study: The insightfulness that serves as the key discipline for the spiritual journey includes a willingness to receive what we see. That is, we must commit ourselves to God in such a way that we are open to whatever God is doing in the world. We must receive the *basileia* like children, like those not invested in the power structures of our day. Consider how, in Mark's story, the heavens were ripped open, the Spirit descended into Jesus, and God was on the loose in our realm (1:10–11)! Consider how Jesus said we do not know the time of God's *basileia* (13:33)–its coming is unexpected and surprising. God's Spirit unloosed for surprising work in our world will likely not be concerned to fit into our time frames, chosen places of power, or sense of order, or to approve our guest lists. Instead, the Spirit will be about the will of God, however unexpected God's will may be to us. To *see* God's work, therefore, requires a willingness to receive these unexpected challenges to the way we are sure things have always been and, indeed, ought to be.

In the midst of such challenges, the stories, including Mark's story, also bring us good news. They tell unanticipated tales of a woman who anointed Jesus the Messiah for burial, of Bartimaeus and Jacob, of Nasrudin's wisdom, of the thief in the Sufi story and three holy men praying on an island. They tell us that always there have been those who see God on the loose in the world bringing about transformation and who enable others, often against great odds, to see God as well. They encourage us to realize that allegiance to God means that we see and receive God wherever and whenever God is to be found, even when that is in the most unexpected people and places. They show us that such commitment means we can be the ones in our generation working alongside God to help others *see* that God's *basileia* has drawn near.

Insightfulness in the Twenty-first Century

We have suggested before that if Mark's story has truly portrayed aspects of the human condition, we would find it still being relevant for twenty-first–century people.

Probably little else needs to be said for us to appreciate how "on target" these *good* stories, including Mark's story, are to those of us reading a book such as this one. Many of us would likely be considered among the most religious people of our day. Many of us aspire to religious leadership in one form or another. Mark's story warns us that we, despite our religious appearances, can be among those most blind or most closed to what God is doing in the world. Mark's story asks if our allegiance is to God, or to what we want God to do for us, or to our own religious systems and structures that serve us well. The story asks if we are open to seeing God at work bringing about God's will in surprising ways and through unexpected people and circumstances.

Our history, even our recent history, has many examples of religious leaders who pledged allegiance more to self than to God. The damage they caused warns us to take the stories' questions seriously. For instance, many among us today lament how often Protestant missionary activity and Western imperialism worked hand in hand as many religious leaders sought expanded power and influence for themselves and their church structures.[23] Such power-grabbing by missionaries as well as by other religious figures prompted one novelist recently to write the following:

> "I thought religions were supposed to be about love." Her voice was tough and angry. I shrugged sympathetically. I

didn't get the connection but I disagreed with her. To my mind organized religion was about love in roughly the same way that the Mafia was about family. Not. "But [she said] religions are really about power and money and making people do things, things that maybe aren't even the best choice for them."[24]

In terms of seeing God at work bringing about God's will in the most unexpected people and circumstances, our reading of Mark suggests that the church should be leading the struggle to end racial, ethnic, economic, gender, and religious oppression. We should lead this struggle because we see God's acceptance and compassion for all people and God's desire that we live the discipleship of equals. Thankfully, some people in the church have practiced God's compassion for all people. But too many churches, perhaps especially those of middle-class North American Protestant denominations, have served as last bastions of the status quo.

So urban white churches move to the suburbs because "those people" (i.e., homeless people) make them uncomfortable. But where do the stories say God is present and at work? In the most unexpected people, the most unexpected circumstances. So, I am reminded of the board member of Southern Baptist Theological Seminary in Louisville, who said in the documentary *The Battle for the Minds* that those who believe God would call a woman to be a pastor need to go elsewhere to seminary "because we're not going to believe that here." The force with which he spoke makes one wonder what he would say if God used the divine finger to write on the wall, "Let the women preach my word and do not stop them" (compare Mark 10:14). Would he say even then, "We are not going to believe that here"? In his religious system—equated with God?—only men can occupy pulpits. But where is God present and at work? In the most unexpected people, the most unexpected circumstances. So I suspect the last place gays and lesbians can hope to be treated as loved children of God is in many of our churches. But where is God present and at work? In the most unexpected people, the most unexpected circumstances.

Furthermore, isn't there an element of egocentricity in any unwillingness to see God present in unexpected people, just as the stories suggest? A hard truth to face is that many of us enjoy the superior feeling we get from believing we are not like "them," we are more moral than "them," we are higher class than "them," we are better than "them." Many of us can recall Jesus' story of the

Pharisee and the tax collector. The Pharisee prayed, "O God, I thank you that I am not like other people: those who prey on others, those who are unjust, adulterers, or even as this tax collector" (Luke 18:10–13). Well, what would it do to this Pharisee to realize that he *is* like other people, and that other people are just like him? What would it do to us?

Churches and individuals who are seeking expanded power and superior positions for themselves and who are serving as last bastions of the status quo will lack the insightfulness necessary for the spiritual journey. For they are not going to open themselves to seeing God in the most unexpected people or circumstances. They are not going to receive the *basileia* as children. But good stories, as Megan McKenna tells us, are all about disturbing the status quo.[25] So they keep challenging us to see where our allegiance genuinely lies. Surely the offer of such a stiff challenge is a signal that a story is relevant to our contemporary situation: An old story, one of our sacred stories, is still telling us something important about ourselves. Let us see again, therefore, how well Mark understood and portrayed the human condition, and let us learn from it.

Concluding Thoughts

Mark's call to see is woven through the stories in the gospel of those who see and those who do not. The basis of the call to see—the insistence that things are not always what they appear to be—is justified in these stories. The most unlikely people "get it," while the most religious people in the story are the most problematic for Jesus' work.

In telling these stories, Mark also adds to our understanding of the insightfulness that is the key discipline for journeying on the Way of the Lord: It includes an openness to receive what we see. The unexpected ones see that the *basileia* of God has drawn near, and they receive it as children, that is, as those able to pledge their allegiance wholly to God because they are not invested in gaining power and status for themselves through the systems and structures of their world. Thus, they have "nothing to lose" and are free to follow Jesus on the Way of the Lord. The most religious people in the story appear to try to mix their desire for God with their desire for personal power and status. The result is that they either do not see that God's *basileia* has drawn near, or that they see but do not receive what they see as the work of God. Thus, they cause suffering and even death in the name of God. Many other good stories share variations on this theme.

So at the end of all this, these *good* stories, including Mark's story, leave me, as someone who practices her vocation among those who would be considered the most religious people of our day, wondering: Where is the person, or place, or circumstance we would least expect to find God today? Have we seen God there lately? Have we looked? How willing are we to do so? What do our answers to these questions tell us about where our allegiance lies?

CHAPTER 4

"Do Not Be Afraid, Only Believe"
(Mark 5:36)

NEAR THE END of Dante's journey through Purgatory, the day was passing away when God's glad angel appeared to us. He was standing outside the flames on the bank and singing, "Blessed are the pure" in a voice beyond all mortal music. "Blessed souls, you cannot go any farther until the fire bites you first; go on in and don't be deaf to the singing beyond," he said to us when we drew close to him; and when I heard him say this, I felt like someone laid in the grave. I bent forward over my clasped hands, gazing at the fire...My kind escorts turned to me, and Virgil said, "My son, this may mean suffering, but not death. Remember, remember...If I guided you safely on Geryon, what shall I do now nearer to God? Believe me, if you stayed a thousand years in the middle of these flames, they could not burn one hair of your head...Leave behind now, leave behind your fear, and come in confidently." But I wouldn't budge, in spite of my conscience.[1]

_____ Dante, _Purgatory_

WHILE JESUS WAS STILL SPEAKING, some people from the synagogue ruler's house came saying, "Your daughter has died. Why trouble the teacher any longer?" But Jesus, having overheard what they said, said to the synagogue ruler, "Do not be afraid, only believe."

_____ MARK 5:35–36

What these two stories have in common is fear. What we have in common with these two stories is fear. Parker Palmer believes that fear is a contemporary cultural trait at work in every area of our common life. Such a trait may not be readily acknowledged, however. A psychologist friend suspects there is a societal agreement that our fear be kept secret because many people consider fear a shameful sign of inadequacy. But the secrecy does not change the reality. We practice a politics of fear in which candidates are elected by playing on voters' anxieties about race and class or the future of Social Security. We do business in an economy of fear that technology will make our jobs obsolete, in which getting and spending are driven by fears that we cannot keep up with neighbors. We build gated communities to keep out "those people" whom we fear. We subscribe to religions of fear that exploit our dread of death and damnation. Fear, says Palmer, has become the very air we breathe.[2]

Fear is also an ever-present element in journey stories. Dante must walk through a wall of fire to pass over into Paradise. But he is so afraid he feels "like someone laid in a grave." Frodo and his companions, Jumping Mouse, and John Bunyan's Christian are all deeply afraid at various times on their journeys. Thus, the stories tell us that those who undertake the spiritual journey will face fear—there can be no sharing in societal secrets on this road. In a key moment in the second _Star Wars_ movie, _The Empire Strikes Back_ (itself a journey story), Luke Skywalker confidently tells Master Yoda, "I am not afraid." Yoda flattens his ears, narrows his eyes, thrusts his face toward Luke, and responds in a low-pitched, terrible voice, "You _will_ be. You _will_ be."

We are addressing fear in this chapter because fear is also a significant motif in Mark's gospel. The Greek noun for _fear_ and the verb for _be afraid_ (the root of both is _phob-_, from which we get our word _phobia_) occur thirteen times in Mark's gospel, beginning in 4:41 and occurring at key moments in the story. Mark often juxtaposes fear with faith, as in Jesus' words to the synagogue ruler that form the title of this chapter. Some scholars believe that fear is _always_ theological in Mark. Given the prominence of fear in Mark, *good* stories, and our culture, and given that we are studying Mark with the help of these stories in order to be more authentically human in our living today, it makes sense for us to see what Mark will teach us about our fear. So in this chapter we will examine the fear motif throughout Mark. With the help of the stories, we will see the kinds of fear at work in Mark. With their help we will explore which responses to fear enable people to be more authentically human, and which may cause us to turn from the journey and actually participate with evil. Then we will ask specifically about contemporary relevance. What is Mark calling us, in a culture in which fear is the air we breathe, to be and do?

Healthy Fear

As Edward Thornton writes, "feeling weak and vulnerable in the world is not neurotic; it's realistic. Human beings are weak and vulnerable."[3] Consequently, we feel threatened in a variety of ways, and we become afraid. If we give it appropriate attention, fear is actually quite healthy for us. We want our kids to be afraid to cross streets without looking first for cars. But we don't want them to be so afraid that they won't cross a street at all. As a professor, my fear that a topic may create tension in my classroom may be a signal that an issue needs to be brought into the open and discussed. It may also be a warning that I must broach the subject carefully. Too little attention to my fear might lead me to raise the issue carelessly. Too much fear might cause me not to raise it at all. So fear is an innate human response to situations of threat. It is understandable. It is often quite helpful. Frankly, Little Red Riding Hood would have been better served if she had had more fear of the Big Bad Wolf than she had.

Often, therefore, when we encounter another's fear, we understand it so well that it arouses our sympathy. This happens when we come to Mark's tenth chapter and find that Jesus and company were "on the way, going up to Jerusalem" and that those who were following him were afraid (10:32). We who have been reading the story closely commiserate with the fearful ones. Jesus' followers may not have seen the possibility of a discipleship of equals in the *basileia* of God. Apparently, however, even they could not miss the growing hostility directed toward Jesus by the religious leaders of their day. After being bested by Jesus in a dispute in a synagogue, Pharisees and Herodians in Galilee plotted to kill him (3:1–6). Scribes who came down to Galilee from Jerusalem publicly declared him possessed by Beelzebul (3:22) and charged that he taught people not to live according to the tradition of the elders (7:5). Jesus, for his part, publicly accused the religious leaders of blaspheming the Holy Spirit (3:29) and of hypocrisy for rejecting the commands of God to keep their human traditions (7:6–13). That was just in Galilee! Now they were "on the way," going up to Jerusalem where the "big boys" of the religious and political power structure awaited him. Twice already Jesus had said he would die there. So his followers were afraid. No kidding! Who wouldn't be? We understand and sympathize.

There is another instance of Jesus' followers being afraid on the way to Jerusalem, however, that seems to arouse a different response. When Jesus told his followers for the second time that he was going to die and after three days rise again, they did not understand what he was telling them. But they did not ask him to explain further because they were afraid (9:31–32).

In many ways their fear here is also understandable. So often before they had not understood Jesus and had either asked him to explain or betrayed their ignorance in other ways. Each time he was unable or unwilling to hide his disappointment. We've already noted his response to their misunderstanding of his warning against "the yeast of the Pharisees and of Herod" (8:14–21). There were other such moments, such as when he stilled a storm and asked them, "Why are you such cowards? Have you no faith?" (4:40). Or when they did not grasp his teaching that holiness is about pure hearts rather than clean hands, and he said, "Are *you* also without understanding?" (7:18). Or when Peter rebuked Jesus for saying he was going to die, and Jesus called him Satan (8:33). Probably most of us know the feeling of disappointing someone who matters a great deal to us. It is *not* a good feeling. So we understand the disciples being afraid to ask for further explanation that would show Jesus again that they did not "get it." We even sympathize again, and yet...

Why is there an "and yet" here? Why does the disciples' fear during this part of their journey with Jesus make us uncomfortable? Maybe because we find ourselves wondering: because they are afraid to ask, does that mean they should not ask? This question presents us with a means to a further understanding of fear in our lives. It pushes us to examine how fear can be something other than healthy, understandable, and sympathetic.

Fear That Leads to Quitting the Journey

When fear is intense enough, it presses our panic buttons, prompting the response many of us describe as "fight or flight." In the key moments of our lives (for we are not talking here about scurrying back to the curb when we see a car coming), a decision to respond to fear by fleeing causes us to run from mystery, freeze our spontaneity, retreat into ego control, and try to master our own fate. A decision to fight launches a power struggle toward the same end. We try to predict and control the world. We want to replace mystery with mastery. Such actions as these hinder the spiritual journey. They do not allow us to open ourselves to receive whatever God is doing in the world, to see through the illusions all around us, or to follow Jesus wherever he is going "on the way." Thus, Thornton boldly asserts: "When fear prevails in a decision-making process you are seeing the face of evil."[4]

From this perspective the answer to our question above is no. Jesus' followers' fear should *not* have kept them from asking Jesus to explain further. They would never understand if they remained quiet about their lack of understanding. But are we actually seeing the face of evil in their fear-based decision not to ask? What do the subsequent actions of Judas and Peter suggest? Certainly Judas' betrayal of Jesus must give us pause.

Fear and the Religious Leaders in Mark

If we examine the fear of the religious leaders in Mark's story, we will find further reason to take seriously the consequences of allowing fear to prevail in decision making. Three times Mark tells us the religious leaders were afraid. The first time is after Jesus cursed the temple and declared that those involved in the economic enterprises there had turned the "house of prayer for all nations" into a "den of robbers" (11:15–17). The religious leaders then "sought how to kill him, for *they feared him,* for the crowd was astounded at his teaching" (11:18). The next day the religious leaders asked Jesus by what authority he had done these things (in the temple). Jesus responded with a question of his own: From whence did John the Baptist's authority derive (11:27–30)? As we noted in the last chapter, the religious leaders discussed among themselves how to answer. They did not want to say John's authority was from God, for then Jesus would ask why they had not believed John. But they also did not want to say it was from humans, for "*they feared the crowd,* for all said that John truly was a prophet" (11:32). When they finally answered, "We do not know," Jesus then refused to answer their question. Immediately then he told the parable of the workers in the vineyard (12:1–11). The religious leaders knew he told this parable against them, so "they sought to grab hold of him, but *they feared the crowd*" (12:12).

Interesting, isn't it? Once we are told the religious leaders feared Jesus because of his impact on the crowd. Two other times we are simply told they were afraid of the crowd. The crowd, then, is the key factor in their fearfulness. What might we learn by pondering their fear of the crowd?

Understanding the Religious Leaders' Fear

Parker Palmer has observed the following about fears we often experience. We fear diversity, he says. We fear "the other" who is different. We prefer to believe we live in a homogeneous universe so that we can maintain the illusion that we possess the truth about our world and ourselves. If we admit that others have different standpoints, different experiences, different ways of being in the world, then our sense of truth may begin to feel fragile. We fear the conflict that could ensue when these differences meet, because we fear only one perspective can win. The "losing side" is then defeated and may be shamed. What if that side is ours? We fear such a loss because so often we have identified ourselves with our ideas and beliefs about the way the world is and the way it should be. So, in such a conflict, we risk more than losing the contest—we risk losing our sense of self.[5]

Dostoevsky's story of "The Grand Inquisitor" illustrates Palmer's perspective. Since this story is told from the perspective of the cardinal who headed the Inquisition in sixteenth-century Spain—indeed, most of the story is in his own words—there is no explicit reference to his fearing Jesus. He would never admit any such fear. But there are signals that he is afraid. He arrests Jesus immediately upon seeing him with the people. "Why did you come here, to interfere and make things difficult for us?...For You came to interfere—You know it," he says to Jesus, not once but several times. Near the end of the story, "the old man longs for [Jesus] to say something, however painful and terrifying. But instead, He suddenly goes over to the old man and kisses him gently on his old, bloodless lips. And that is His only answer. The old man is startled and shudders."[6] These hints, plus the tone of fearfulness throughout the narrative, suggest the cardinal is very afraid. Thus, his lengthy explanation of his "religious service" offered in the midst of his fear of Jesus is very enlightening.

For example, Jesus was wrong to refuse when Satan tempted him to turn stones into bread, the cardinal declared,

> "For there has never been anything more difficult for [humanity] and for human society to bear than freedom!...But You did not want to deprive [humanity] of freedom and You rejected this suggestion, for, You thought, what sort of freedom would they have if their obedience was bought with bread?...In the end it is *to us* that they will come...and they will beg us: 'Give us food, for those who promised us fire from heaven have not given it to us!' And that will be the day when *we shall finish building their tower* [of Babel] for them, for the one who feeds them will be the one who finishes building it, and we will be the only ones capable of feeding them. And we shall give them bread in Your name and lie, telling them that it is in Your name. *Oh, never, never would they be able to feed themselves without us!*"[7]

Jesus was also wrong to refuse "all the kingdoms of the world" that Satan offered him, according to the cardinal:

> "You could have taken Caesar's sword when You came the last time...Had You [done so] You would have fulfilled [humanity's] greatest need on earth. That is, the need to find someone to worship, someone who can relieve [them] of the burden of [their] conscience, thus enabling [them] finally to unite into *a harmonious ant-hill where there are no dissenting voices...We* accepted Rome and Caesar's sword from [Satan]."[8]

Bearing this sword is a burdensome job, the cardinal insisted, but it is necessary because Jesus made such a disastrous mistake. Jesus gave people their freedom. But they are too weak, corrupt, worthless, and restless to be free! Jesus should have respected people less and thus demanded less of them—"that would have been more like love."[9] Instead Jesus created a situation where "freedom, free-thinking, and science" lead people into such dilemmas and confusion that they destroy one another as well as themselves. So the cardinal and his associates are cleaning up the mess Jesus created when he set people free to explore life, the world, and themselves.

"*The herd will be gathered together and tamed* again, however, and this time for good…Oh, we shall have to convince them, finally, that they must not be proud, for, by overestimating them, You instilled pride in them. We shall prove to them that they are nothing but weak, pathetic children, but that a child's happiness is the sweetest of all…They will admire us, be terrified of us, and be proud of the strength and wisdom that enabled us to subdue a turbulent herd of many millions."[10]

Once upon a time the cardinal himself had faithfully followed Jesus. He had lived in the wilderness, fed on roots and locusts, and blessed the freedom that Jesus gave to human beings. He was prepared "to take my place among the strong, chosen ones, aspiring to be counted among them. But I came to my senses and refused to serve a mad cause. I turned away and joined those who were endeavoring to *correct Your work*."[11] So, at the end of the story the old man walks to the door, opens it, and says to Jesus, "Go now, and do not come back…ever. You must never, never come back again!"[12]

We find Palmer's description of reasons we fear vividly portrayed in this story. Let us begin where Palmer ended, with one's sense of self, that is, with ego concerns. We cannot help but notice the cardinal's focus on himself and those who are with him. In today's parlance, "it's all about us." The people "admire *us,* are terrified of *us,*" he says. They could never, never "feed themselves *without us.*" Even when he mentions the time of his "faithful following" of Jesus, he says he did so "to take *my place* among the strong, chosen ones, aspiring to be counted among them." All along he insists *he* knows what is best for people. So he is "correcting Jesus' work" by taking people's freedom from them for their own good. The poor wretches have been trying to build their own tower of Babel. But they are too weak and pathetic, so "*we* shall finish building their tower for them, for the one who feeds them will be the one who finishes building it, and *we* will be the only ones capable of feeding them."

Do we see in the cardinal's egocentricity the source of his fear of Jesus? Let us note that if Jesus' very different message of freedom took hold in people, they would no longer admire the cardinal, be terrified of him, be proud of his "strength and wisdom," or go tamely into the harmonious anthill he envisions where there are no dissenting voices. Nor could the cardinal continue with his plans to complete his tower of Babel, which is itself a telling reference. The first builders of Babel intended a tower with a "top in the heavens" so as to "make a name" for themselves (Gen. 11:4). So with his egocentricity swelling like those of the ancient Babel builders, the cardinal fears any conflict in which people would choose between Jesus' message and his own. He has invested too much of himself in his view of the world, his view of people, and his ambitions (i.e., his "tower") to risk defeat. Acting out of his fear, he arrests Jesus immediately, thus halting any conflict before it starts, and tells Jesus to "never, never come back again."

When I look at Palmer's perspective on fear and at "The Grand Inquisitor" in this way, I cannot help but think of the religious leaders in Mark's story. We learned in the last chapter that they had pledged their allegiance to their positions, power, and privilege–to ego concerns. They operate and control the religious-political-economic system that is centered in the temple, and they may even equate their system with God. They are fully invested in serving this God, for this God has served them well. If this analysis of the religious leaders is correct, far more than the job by which they feed their families is at stake in their conflict with Jesus. Their sense of self and God is wrapped up in their authority to administer the temple system. If the crowd follows Jesus and ignores *their* teaching on purity and holiness and who is worthy to draw near to God; if the crowd stops bringing their tithes and taxes to the temple; if they curse the temple as a den of robbers and pray for it to be cast into the sea; if they no longer salute the religious leaders in the marketplace or give them the best seats in the synagogue or places of honor at feasts; if the crowd believes the religious leaders are hypocrites, then who are they anymore? How can the religious leaders keep their power and place at the top of the pyramid? How can they maintain the lifestyle to which they have become accustomed and perhaps believe is their right? For all these reasons, they fear the crowd, and they fear Jesus because of his impact on the crowd. Thus, acting out of their fear, they arrest Jesus and conspire with the Romans to execute him.

Right about here we should return to Palmer's teaching and remember that he is describing fears that are, frankly, ordinary. Any of us fear differences that can lead to conflict that might lead to shame and loss of our sense of self. When Jumping Mouse is the only mouse who wants to journey to the Sacred Mountains, he must leave his community behind. He travels across the Plains, where there are eagles who will try to kill him for food before he arrives at his journey's end. Along the way he gives up parts of himself. At the end he must yield his very self. Consequently, he is always afraid in the story. How could he not be? Any of us can understand and sympathize with his fear. No, the fear itself is not the problem.

The key concern instead is our response to our fear. Let us note again the assertion that when fear prevails in decision making—when we choose to run from mystery, retreat into ego-control, and seek to master the world around us—we are seeing the face of evil. Clearly fear has prevailed in the decision making in the stories we have been considering. So do we see the face of evil when the Grand Inquisitor arrests Jesus and sends him away? when the religious leaders in Mark arrest Jesus and conspire to execute him? Surely we do! Furthermore, both these stories, one of which is a sacred story for us Christians, illustrate that a primary allegiance to ego-concerns leads to fear prevailing in decision making, which leads to evil being done. The whole evil sequence begins with ego-centeredness. Thus, there is a key lesson here for those of us longing to be authentically human, as God created us to be.

Fear among Other Characters in Mark

The minor characters in Mark's story show us another kind of fear that impacts the spiritual journey. We turn to Mark 5, which tells us Jesus has traveled across the Sea of Galilee, though not without some difficulty (4:35–41, which we'll address shortly), to the country of the Gerasenes. There he is met by a man possessed by a legion of demons. The evil within the man has made him strong and violent. No one can control him, not even with chains and shackles. He lives among the tombs and on the mountains, evidently unclothed, screaming, and bruising himself with stones day and night. What a terror he must have been to the people there! Consequently, when Jesus casts out the demons so that the man is clothed, in his right mind, and sitting with Jesus, we might have expected the people of the region to throw a party. Instead, Mark tells us, when they found the menace removed from their midst, *they were afraid* and begged Jesus to leave their country (5:1–17).

Does this seem an odd reaction? Well, this is not the only biblical story about fear in response to a moment that is filled with grace and gift. In the year that King Uzziah died, Isaiah "saw" the Lord in the temple, high and lofty and sitting on a throne. The building shook and filled with smoke while seraphs sang praises to God. Isaiah responded, "Woe is me! I am lost, for I am a man of unclean lips, and I live among a people of unclean lips; yet my eyes have seen the King, the LORD of hosts!" (Isa. 6:5). Though the word "afraid" does not appear in this text, Isaiah's "Woe is me! I am lost" is surely an expression of the fear he felt in the moment. Similarly, Peter reacted to a miraculous catch of fish prompted by Jesus' word by falling at Jesus' knees and saying, "Go away from me for I am a sinful man, Lord" (Luke 5:8). We suspect that fear is the reason Peter would push Jesus away. When Jesus tells him, "Do not be afraid" (5:10), we are sure.

Nor are these biblical stories the only *good* stories about this kind of fear. When Rat and Mole go seeking a lost baby otter in Kenneth Grahame's *The Wind in the Willows,* they unexpectedly hear a beautiful "song-dream." They follow it in their boat to an island in their river that turns out to be a holy place. There,

> the Mole felt a great Awe fall upon him, an awe that turned his muscles to water, bowed his head, and rooted his feet to the ground. It was no panic terror...but it was an awe that smote and held him and, without seeing, he knew it could only mean that some august Presence was very, very near. With difficulty he turned to look for his friend, and saw him at his side cowed, stricken, and trembling violently.[13]

A moment later in the story the two encounter the character who is named "the Friend and Helper." Mole asks Rat if he is afraid. "'Afraid?' murmured the Rat, his eyes shining with unutterable love. 'Afraid! Of *Him*? O, never, never! And yet–and yet–O, Mole, I am afraid!"[14]

The prevalence of fear before an "august Presence" in these stories–even though in each instance the Presence offers grace– suggests such fear is intrinsic to the human condition. Twentieth-century thinkers agree. Philosopher Rudolf Otto wrote of the awful, dreadful, fascinating attraction we feel during an experience of tremendous mystery.[15] Palmer claims that one of our deepest fears is of a live encounter with what he calls "alien otherness."[16] Poet Kathleen Norris describes the "holy fear" that makes us feel small "in the face of God's vastness, God's might, God's being."[17] Sometimes we think of this fear as awe, as Kenneth Grahame writes in his story, and certainly it is. But I am struck that the Bible (and other *good* stories also) consistently speaks of people being afraid during these encounters. This consistency suggests there is something genuinely terrifying about being in the presence of the divine Other.

We can turn to a story of the disciples in Mark for a further example of this fear. After teaching all day in parables (4:1–34),

Jesus told his followers they should go to the other side of the Sea of Galilee. As they were crossing the sea, a great storm arose—this is the difficult boat trip of 4:35–41 alluded to earlier. Amazingly, Jesus was sleeping through the uproar. His disciples woke him up, saying "Teacher, does it not concern you that we are perishing?" I take their question to be sarcastic and angry. Among the disciples are experienced fishermen who know what to do in a storm, but who also know what hard work storm survival is. Significantly, there is no mention of their being afraid of the storm. Nor did they ask Jesus to save them from the storm when they woke him (as in Matthew and perhaps implicitly in Luke). Instead, they were angry that he was sleeping while they were working so hard to keep the boat afloat. Apparently they wanted him to take his place in the bucket brigade.

Rather than pick up a bucket, however, Jesus rebuked the wind and said to the sea, "Be calm! Hush!" And they did! *Now* we are told the disciples are afraid. Indeed, Mark says "they feared a great fear" as they wondered, "Who is this that even the wind and the sea obey him?" Their question, however, is quite rhetorical. The disciples' fear is not a result of not knowing who Jesus is. In the Jewish tradition, only God can still the raging sea (note Job 26:12; Isa. 51:15; Jer. 31:35; Ps. 89:9–10; Ps. 107:29).[18] Therefore, they understand Jesus' identity clearly, or more precisely, they understand who is at work in Jesus. That is why they are afraid, for Jesus is, as poet Mary Oliver has written,

> tender and luminous and demanding
> as he always was—
> *a thousand times more frightening*
> *than the killer sea.*[19]

Understanding Their Fear

This fear is prominent in biblical stories and other *good* stories. Yet it seems today that we have scant awareness of it. Norris senses "much fear of fear itself in the contemporary landscape." In our "fear of fear," she says, we have lost the ancient sense of fear as reverence and wonder and so "are left with only the negative connotations of the word."[20] Thus, we rarely hear any discussion of God's presence as terrifying. We memorize and recite Psalm 23 ("the LORD is my shepherd"). We read over hurriedly, if at all, verses such as Hebrews 12:29 ("for our God is fire which consumes"). But the stories, including Mark's story, keep telling us of the fear of God's presence that comes naturally to us human beings.

I have no desire to minimize the comforting experience of the presence of God, who is gracious and merciful, slow to anger and abounding in steadfast love. I am suggesting instead that we *have been minimizing* the fearful aspect of the experience of the holy. Let's give our attention to this fear, therefore, and ask: What is so terrifying about a close encounter with God, who is, after all, our good Shepherd?

If we take seriously our affirmation that God is light, truth, and even consuming fire, we must acknowledge that entering God's presence will necessarily expose the ragged edges of our lives and how our neatly ordered worlds are not so neat and not so orderly. Consider how the encounter with the Holy exposed the lies of Isaiah's life, Peter's sinfulness, and the Grand Inquisitor's egocentric service of Satan. Are we ready to have this kind of experience with God's Light and Truth? Are we ready to *see* whether or not we have pledged primary allegiance to our egos? Are we ready to *see* whether or not we have loved God for self's sake? Are we ready to *see* whether or not the religious, political, and economic systems that are operative in our world, which may be serving us well, have exploited and marginalized people who are "other" than us? Because if we see that people are being exploited, we will have to decide if we are going to receive what we see. That is, will we change our lives and give up our privileged positions because we have committed ourselves to God and cannot cooperate with such systems? If we do so, we are likely to be opposed by those who support the systems— are we ready for such experiences? In other words, are we ready to deny self, take up our crosses, and follow Jesus "on the way of the Lord?" Or do we prefer to go on living with our illusions about ourselves and our world?

No wonder, then, that the stories talk about our "fear" of God, for an encounter with the divine presence will inevitably call us to be transformed. We will be challenged, maybe even compelled, to change our lives. That, says Palmer, is the most daunting threat of all.[21]

Right about here we should remind ourselves again that we are describing fear that is, in a sense, ordinary. Any of us fear exposure. Indeed, how many of us have dreamed of showing up somewhere stark naked and have awakened with pounding hearts? That's fear of exposure! Furthermore, change usually induces fear in us. Again, the fear itself is not wrong. It is simply part of the human condition. No, the issue again is, how do we respond to our fear? In the story of the Gerasene people in Mark 5, fear prevailed in their decision making. They saw the demon-possessed man sitting with Jesus, clothed and in his right mind, and they were afraid. So they begged Jesus to go away. A power that could heal such a man promised them more Light and Truth than they were ready for. Consequently, they pushed that power away.

Do we have much in common with the Gerasenes? Is fear prevailing in our decisions about how we respond to God because the divine presence promises more Light and Truth than we are ready for? If so, we will run away from mystery. We will retreat into ego-control. These actions—running from and retreating—are obviously opposite of traveling forward on the spiritual journey. They cause us not to be human, as God created us to be.

Journeying Forward with Our Fear

We have noted that fear is a basic human emotion. We are going to be afraid when threatened. We have seen that human beings fear an encounter with the "other" that could lead to conflict, that could lead to loss of our sense of self. We have also seen that we fear the near presence of God because that presence exposes us. Since we are going to be afraid, how can we be able not to have these fears determine our decisions so that we journey forward rather than retreat?

Learning from Mark's Insightful Minor Characters

We get a lesson here from another of Mark's minor characters. After the Gerasene people sent Jesus away, he crossed to the other side of the sea. There he was met by Jairus, a synagogue ruler whose daughter was dying. Jesus said yes to his pleas for help and journeyed with him to his home (5:21–24). Mark then interrupts this story to introduce us to a woman in the crowd around Jesus who was suffering from a twelve-year "flow of blood."

Mark gives us much detail about her situation. We become aware of the seeming hopelessness of her physical condition—after years of seeing doctors she was worse rather than better. We can sense her social and religious isolation—her flow of blood would have made her unclean. We are told of the economic disaster she faced—she had spent all she had on doctors. And we know that she had been enduring these circumstances for twelve years (5:25–26). So when Mark tells us that she took matters into her own hands, waded into the crowd where her uncleanness would have made her unwelcome, touched Jesus' clothes, and was healed immediately (5:27–29), we readers are prepared to grasp the magnitude of the moment. The enormity of it certainly did not escape her. Mark tells us she *feared* and trembled because she knew what had happened to her (5:33).

Meanwhile Jesus had stopped in the midst of the procession to Jairus' home because he wanted to *see* who had touched him. He looked around for who had done it (5:30–32). The woman came forward to tell him. When the Gerasenes had encountered a power that could heal their demon-possessed man, they were afraid and begged Jesus to *go away*. He did so. When the woman encountered a power that could heal her impossible disease, she was afraid and *came forward* to Jesus to tell him the whole truth of the moment (5:33). He blessed her for it (5:34). The contrasting movement in these two stories is telling.

But just in case we are acting like the Twelve and not "getting it," Mark returns to Jairus' story and gives us a second look at responding to our fear. As Jesus was blessing the woman, word reached them that Jairus' daughter had died. "Why trouble the teacher further?" the people from Jairus' house asked. But Jesus said to Jairus, "Do not be afraid; only believe" (5:36). At first glance, Jesus' words may seem odd. We might have expected "do not grieve," or "do not give up hope." Instead he says, "Do not be afraid." A power that stills a storm (4:35–41), casts out a legion of demons (5:1–13), and heals a twelve-year hemorrhage (5:25–34), which is the power of the presence of God, is about to enter Jairus' house and raise his daughter from death (5:40–42). No wonder, then, that Jesus says, "Do not be afraid."

Not Being Our Fears

Palmer offers an insightful "midrash" on Jesus' counsel to Jairus. It is important to note, he says, what Jesus did not say. Jesus did not say that "we should not *have* fears"–and if he had, we could dismiss his word "as an impossible counsel of perfection." Instead Jesus' words tell us "we do not have to *be* our fears." We will be afraid of opposition, of transformation, of threats to our sense of self, of journeying through the wilderness, even of God. But, Palmer says, we do not have to be dominated by our fears.[22] Storyteller John Shea observes that fears will be companions on our journeys, but they need not become "vigilant, sleepless guards on the walls of the prisons we have made for ourselves."[23] Kathleen Norris reminds us that our fear of God can encourage our journeys, for it allows us to recognize that the Holy One is in our midst. It may be painful to see our lives and our world in the light of God's presence. But only when we see, says Norris, are we able "to let God awaken in us capacities and responsibilities we have been afraid to contemplate."[24] It is possible, therefore, to understand such encounters with God as something that enriches our lives.

Perhaps the story that best illustrates not *being* our fears happens near the end of Mark's account of Jesus' journey. In Gethsemane, alone and in the dark, with his soul "grieving unto death," Jesus prayed that "this hour would pass," that God would take "this cup" from him (14:35–36). As we have seen, Jesus' travels on "the way of the Lord," announcing and making visible the *basileia* of God, aroused intense opposition from those invested in the old ways. Now he had journeyed all the way to Jerusalem, the symbolic place of God's presence with the people, to give the religious leaders a last chance to receive what they saw. Out of their fear they refused. For Jesus to continue on this way, therefore, would mean his death.

So in Gethsemane he was afraid and longed for permission to quit this journey. This moment was the "dark night of the soul" for Jesus in Mark, the moment when he must finally decide between self-preservation (i.e., ego concerns) or self-transcendence (i.e., committing himself to something larger than himself). One choice is surely safer and easier. But it is limiting. The other choice is frightening, but involves being part of what God is doing in the world. Mark shows us Jesus' decision by recording his famous words, "Not what *I* will, but what *you* will" (14:36). Not ego-concerns, but God. Jesus' fear was very real, but it did not prevail in his decision making. He was not dominated by his fears–he did not become his fears. How very different from the religious leaders, the Grand Inquisitor, the Gerasene people!

Only Believe

The Gethsemane story shows us still more. It underscores for us *how* we are able not to be our fears and to journey forward. We do so by having pledged our allegiance ultimately to God, not to self. Back in Mark 5 Jesus' words to Jairus were not only "do not be afraid." They were also "only believe." That is, only believe in God. Only commit our way to the way of the Lord. Not our will, but God's. Trust that the journey to which we have been called leads us home to ourselves.

Good stories affirm and illustrate Mark's "do not be afraid, only believe." Dante, in the story at the beginning of this chapter, finally believed the guide sent to him from Paradise—"A voice singing on the other side of the fire guided us through, and *by concentrating on it* we emerged where the ascent began."[25] Jumping Mouse was so frightened along his journey that he almost turned back. On his way, for example, he came to the prairie where there were many eagles. "But he was determined to go to the Sacred Mountains. He gathered all of his courage and ran just as fast as he could out onto the prairie. His little heart pounded with excitement and fear." He met a dying buffalo who could only be saved by the eye of a mouse. Jumping Mouse gave him one of his. In return the buffalo told Jumping Mouse to run under his belly across the rest of the prairie so the eagles could not see him. Jumping Mouse trusted him. So they ran toward the mountains with Jumping Mouse "secure and hidden from the [eagles], but with only one eye it was frightening." At the foot of the mountains the buffalo left him. Then Jumping Mouse met a wolf who had lost his memory. He gave his other eye to heal the wolf. In return the wolf said he would take Jumping Mouse to the Great Medicine Lake in the Sacred Mountains. Though blind and fearful, Jumping Mouse believed him. When they arrived, the wolf described the lake's beauty while Jumping Mouse drank from the water. Then the wolf left to guide others to this place.

> Jumping Mouse sat there trembling in fear. It was no use running, for he was blind, but he knew an eagle would find him there. He felt a shadow on his back and heard the sound eagles make. He braced himself for the shock. And the eagle hit! Jumping Mouse went to sleep. Then he woke up. The surprise of being alive was great, but now he could see.[26]

Jumping Mouse also had a new name—he was Eagle! As John Shea comments, Jumping Mouse was always afraid. Rather than allowing his fear to become master of a barricaded house from which he never moved, however, he took it with him on his journey to the Sacred Mountains.[27]

Have you given thought to the story of Ebenezer Scrooge lately? Consider the reaction of Scrooge to the ghost of Jacob Marley, who came to see him on Christmas Eve night. He insisted to the ghost that his senses were easily affected by an upset stomach: "You may be an undigested bit of beef, a blot of mustard, a crumb of cheese, a fragment of an underdone potato. There's more of gravy than of grave about you, whatever you are." In reality, Scrooge sought to be funny to distract himself and keep "his terror down, for the specter's voice disturbed the very marrow of his bones."[28] Marley announced that three Spirits would visit Scrooge to give him the chance to escape Marley's tortured existence after death. Scrooge responds he'd rather not. But the Spirits come anyway.

So the Ghost of Christmas Past shows Scrooge his joyful little sister, whose surviving son Scrooge treats badly; his early bosses, who dealt with him kindly in contrast to his treatment of Bob Cratchit; and the woman who would not marry him because he loved money most of all. Scrooge calls the visions torture. Next the Ghost of Christmas Present shows Scrooge the Cratchit household eating Christmas dinner with their love, their too-small pudding, and their pain over Tiny Tim's suffering. The Spirit takes him to the jolly Christmas gathering at his nephew's home wherein his nephew toasts Scrooge's health and wishes him a merry Christmas despite Scrooge's ill treatment of him. Finally he shows the two wretched, hideous children of Humanity named Want and Ignorance who horrify Scrooge so. We might wonder if anyone has ever had her or his life more exposed by an experience with an "alien Other" than did Scrooge.

But now, see how Scrooge greeted the third Spirit:

> "Ghost of the future!" he exclaimed, "I fear you more than any other specter I have seen. But as I know your purpose is to do me good, and as I hope to live to be another man from what I was, I am prepared to bear you company, and do it with a thankful heart."…"Lead on!" said Scrooge–"lead on!"[29]

Surely Scrooge's words, "I hope to live to be another man from what I was," strike a chord within those of us who undertake the spiritual journey in hopes of becoming authentically human, as God created us to be. Scrooge understood that to realize his hope, he could not be dominated by his fears. He had to journey forward with–not run away from–that which he feared most. And he could do so because he believed the Spirits' purpose was "to do me good."

So Mark and the stories affirm what we know from personal experience: When our ambitions, positions, ideas, or belief systems are challenged; when our sense of self is threatened; when our ragged edges and egocentricity are exposed by God and "in danger" of transformation, we will be afraid. These fears are part of the human condition. But Mark and the stories also show us that when we believe in Something larger than ourselves, or, in Mark's words, when we have committed ourselves to the Way of the Lord, we are able to choose to follow the will of God even when we are afraid. Then we are able to journey forward when God calls, because our allegiance is finally not to any of these concerns, but to God. Fear does not prevail in our decision making about our lives. We do not become our fears. Instead, we take our fears along for the ride as we believe in God, and we journey toward becoming the persons God created us to be.

So Jesus, alone and afraid in the dark, chose God's will over his own and changed history. Many of us only think at this point about how we can never be like Jesus. Well, let us remember the others. The hemorrhaging woman came to Jesus even while fearing and trembling and received his blessing. Jumping Mouse ran through his fear to the Sacred Mountains, drank from the Great Medicine Lake, and became an eagle. Dante finally believed his guides and walked with his fear through the wall of fire into Paradise. Scrooge welcomed the Spirit he feared most, believing it came to do him good. And he indeed became "another man" than what he had been:

> He became as good a friend, as good a master, and as good a man as the good old City knew, or any other good old city, town, or borough in the good old world. Some people laughed to see the alteration in him, but he let them laugh, and little heeded them…His own heart laughed, and that was quite enough for him.[30]

Fear in the Early Twenty-first Century

Let us return now to Parker Palmer's observation that in our culture today fear is the air we breathe. If he is right, then the relevance for us of Mark's stories about fear ought not be hard to discern. Let us return also to my friend's suggestion that there is a societal agreement to keep our fear secret. If she is correct, then a question arises for us from our study of Mark: Are we willing to *see* through the veil of secrecy? Are we willing to see how afraid we have been, what we are afraid of, what our fear is doing to us, and what we must do in response to our fear if we would become the persons God created us to be?

In reading Mark alongside *good* stories, I am struck by how clearly and how often ego-centeredness is portrayed as irreconcilable with the spiritual journey. In chapter 1 we noted that the mystics understood the illuminative stage of the spiritual journey to be concerned with transcending self-centeredness. We must pass through this stage before we can have genuine communion with God. In chapter 3 we saw that whether we pledge our allegiance to God or to self affects our ability to see or to see and receive what we see. In this chapter we found that our commitment of ourselves to God or to self-concern is a key factor—maybe *the* key factor—in whether or not fear prevails in our decisions about our lives. Here we have discovered that Mark and the stories affirm Palmer's insight that our fears of the Other are finally the result of fearing the loss of our own sense of self. We saw that God's near presence is fearful because God's Light and Truth expose us. We reminded ourselves several times that such fears are quite ordinary. We all fear threats to our sense of self. All of us fear exposure. But what if we have invested ourselves in our sense of self, in our beliefs, ideas, positions, privileges, or ambitions, that is, in our ego concerns? Then should these be threatened, our fear becomes overwhelming because we have so very much to lose. Mark and the stories also affirm that when fear overwhelms our decision making, evil is done.

Obviously, then, this concern about ego-centeredness is an old one, showing up as it does in stories that have been told and retold for generations. But it seems almost unbelievably on target in our time. Contemporary Western culture is so much about pumping up our egos. What we learn from our current cultural obsession with consumption is to be totally selfish. Spiritual director Richard Rohr says our culture teaches that ego is "the only game in town." So we take ourselves too seriously and consider "the private ego as if it is full reality."[31] Hebrew Bible scholar Clinton McCann believes the "American dream" is now defined as "reaching a point in life where you don't have to do anything you don't want to do, where you can be totally self-centered, totally self-directed, accountable to no one but yourself."[32] Psychologist Mary Pipher says we begin learning this focus on self early in our lives. Children are taught through advertising that "they are the most important person in the world," and that their "impulses should not be denied." Add to this mix what she calls the "fuzzy, self-help message that the only commitment is to the self and the only important question is—Am I happy?" So we "catch on" that we are number one and that our own immediate needs are the most important ones. We are socialized to be self-centered. [33] Given this cultural focus on ego-centeredness, and given what Mark and the stories show us about fear rising out of ego-centeredness, is there any wonder that "fear is the air we breathe" today?

Two important caveats should be stressed. First, this critique of egocentricity does not mean that "ego" itself is bad. Many of us today are aware of pain and problems caused by low self-esteem, which sometimes becomes self-negation. Feminist theologians and spirituality teachers have described how particularly harmful self-negation has been for women who have been socialized to live for fathers, husbands, children, bosses, and so forth. Too many women have never learned to identify and express their genuine needs. Too many women have never developed their personalities or gifts or abilities. Too many women have accepted inferiority and even abuse as the price they must pay for being women. But self-negation is harmful to men as well. It can cause any of us to fear the crowd or to hand over our freedom to grand inquisitors and march meekly into harmonious anthills where there are no dissenting voices.

So the second caveat is that the opposite of self-centeredness is not self-negation, but what spiritual teachers call our "true selves." Rohr elaborates: "There is a small 'I' that has to let go so that the true 'I' can be born." The small I wants to fix, name, control, and insure everything for itself—that's self-centeredness. The true self recognizes that "I am in a river that is bigger than I am. The foundation and flow of that river is love. Life is not about me; it's about God." And God is about love.[34] Dorothee Soelle says the spiritual journey takes us to "the farthest point of self-emptying" so that we can "experience the deepest self-confirmation."[35] As far back as the desert fathers and mothers (in the third and fourth centuries), spiritual teachers were emphasizing the goodness of the image of God with which we were born, though it is now hidden by the "muck" of our everyday living. According to church historian Roberta Bondi, these monastics taught that we can rediscover and live out of the conviction that all of us are made in God's image. Then "no one is in a position to look down on another from a superior height because of his or her hard work or piety or mental superiority. We are all vulnerable, all limited, and we each have a different struggle only God is in a position to judge."[36] In the language of this book, the opposite of self-centeredness is being authentically human, as God created us to be.

There is a story, of course, that shows us how we might *see* ourselves truly. It is said that Rabbi Bunam of Pzhysha once told his disciples, "Everyone must have two pockets, so that he can reach into the one or the other, according to his needs. In his right pocket are to be the words 'For my sake the world was created,' and in his left, 'I am earth and ashes.'"[37]

Much of the spiritual journey, then, is about letting go of our self-centeredness and coming home to our true selves. But our self-centeredness (particularly these days when it is so encouraged) and our fear (often the result of our self-centeredness) mean that coming home to ourselves requires major change. Religious folk call this change conversion. Most of us have hidden our egocentricity from ourselves (which is easy to do since it is so normal in this culture). We have believed we are "not like that." We get defensive when someone suggests otherwise. Many of us who consider ourselves religious think we have already been converted. The journey through the dark night of the soul, through the wilderness and Gethsemane, therefore, is fearful because the presence of God exposes how much conversion we still need. We are called to *see* how concerned we've been for keeping up appearances, how addicted to work and achievement we've been, how agenda-driven and lazy and lustful we've been. We are called to *see* how we have sought security in wealth and power and patterns of behavior that are essentially violent. We are called to *see* how vulnerable and wounded and in need of healing we really are. Those of us who consider ourselves religious are called to *see* if we are serving God or ourselves. We are called to abandon our heroic images of ourselves and really *see* ourselves. This is a fearful prospect. Rohr tells us, "You will want to run, I assure you."[38]

Mark and the stories urge us not to run, however much we want to. To be sure, nothing in this culture encourages us to stay the course. It says instead, "Look out for number one," and "I haven't got time for the pain." But Mark and the stories tell us that if we journey forward, taking our fear along as a companion rather than allowing it to stop us; if we believe in God, who has called us to this journey and who exposes us; if we choose God's will over our own, then we can become other than the fearful, self-centered persons we may have been. We will arrive at Paradise, at the Sacred Mountains. We will find ourselves floating in the river whose flow and foundation is love. We will know ourselves to be vulnerable and wounded, but also part of a much larger mystery, part of what God is doing in the world. We will see our world and ourselves with insightfulness. We will see those messages that say happiness is a new car or impressive investments or being impossibly thin for the deceptions they really are. Fear will not prevail in our decision making, so we will resist evil rather than contributing to it. We will have known dark nights of the soul, but we will also know how our hearts can laugh. We will be learning to value ourselves highly as creatures made in God's image, but will understand at the same time that we must not take ourselves too seriously, for we are only earth and ashes. We will have come home to ourselves.

Concluding Thoughts

Jesus' disciples, the religious leaders, the Gerasene people, the hemorrhaging woman, even Jesus himself, knew fear. So did Dante, the Grand Inquisitor, Jumping Mouse, and Scrooge. So do we. We fear how others can threaten our sense of self. We fear God's presence, which exposes the ragged edges of our lives. The more we have invested ourselves in ego concerns, the more our fear of being threatened and exposed intensifies until it overwhelms us. Since this culture is so much about pumping up our egos, there is no wonder fear has become the air we breathe.

When fear overwhelms us, it determines our decisions about our lives and turns us toward doing evil. Mark and the stories tell us of people dominated by their fears and the evils, great and small, they perpetrated. Nonetheless, Mark and the stories bring us good news. Yes, we will be afraid, they tell us. Still, we do not have to become our fears. Like the hemorrhaging woman, we can be afraid *and* come forward into God's presence. If only we commit ourselves to Something larger than ourselves, if only we trust the Way of the Lord to which we have been called, if only we believe in God, then we will not retreat and run away. Instead, we can journey forward to Paradise, we can come home to ourselves even while being afraid, if only we believe. If only.

CHAPTER 5

THE END OF THE STORY

"'There You Will See Him'…They Were Afraid" (Mark 16:7–8)

ONCE UPON A TIME, along the hobbit Frodo's journey to destroy the One Ring that would give the evil lord Sauron all power over Middle-earth, Gandalf the wizard died in battle against a monster. In so doing, he saved the lives of Frodo and his companions. So, alive but more hopeless than ever, the company journeyed on. Bad tidings surrounded them, their suffering increased, their prospects worsened. Then they encountered a frightening old man in Fangorn forest. "There he stood, grown suddenly tall, towering above them. His hood and his grey rags were flung away. His white garments shone. He lifted up his staff, and Gimli's axe leaped from his grasp and fell ringing on the ground. The sword of Aragorn, stiff in his motionless hand, blazed with a sudden fire…They all gazed at him. His hair was white as snow in the sunshine; and gleaming white was his robe; the eyes under his deep brows were bright, piercing as the rays of the sun; power was in his hand. Between wonder, joy, and fear they stood and found no words to say. At last Aragorn stirred. 'Gandalf!' he said. 'Beyond all hope you return to us in our need!'"

TOLKIEN, *THE TWO TOWERS*[1]

ONCE UPON A TIME the powers executed Jesus (just like we knew they would if we have been reading the story). But very early on the first day of the week, as the sun was rising, some of the women, some of those who had not abandoned him, went to anoint his hastily buried body. The first shock they got upon arriving was finding the stone already rolled away from the tomb. The second shock was discovering a young man dressed in white inside the tomb instead of Jesus. The third shock was his words to them: "He has been raised. He is not here. He is going before you into Galilee. There you will *see* him." Then the women ran from the tomb. And they said not one thing to anyone. For they were afraid.

The end.

_____ MARK 16:1–8, PARAPHRASED

Those of us who love stories do not need literary critics to tell us that the way a story ends is crucial for our experience of that story. We know that a bad ending can ruin a good story, a satisfying ending can redeem what had been a frustrating story, a surprising ending can leave us laughing, talking, feeling thrilled, or even screaming (literally or figuratively).

Literary critics do, however, help us understand why endings are so crucial. They tell us that endings are about closure. We want to sense that the narration has reached its goal and is finished, that all the expectations generated along the way by the story itself have been satisfied. When the narrative is appropriately concluded, readers are content that the story does not go on. Whether explicitly or implicitly, ironically or literally, positively or even negatively, we expect our narratives to be coherent and come to closure just as we expect a conundrum to have an answer and a joke a punch line. As literary critic Frank Kermode says, we are in love with fulfillment.[2]

Consequently, Mark's ending has long confounded its readers. First, the words of the young man in 16:6 ("he has been raised, he is not here") satisfy expectations raised earlier by Jesus' predictions of his death and resurrection (8:31; 9:31; 10:33f). Then the young man raises expectations that one final prediction from Jesus will be satisfied: He tells the women that Jesus is "going before you into Galilee; there you will see him just as he said to you" (see 14:28). The coherence and integrity of the story prior to this moment, especially regarding Jesus' predictions and their fulfillment, have prepared readers to expect satisfaction again. We await, perhaps with eager anticipation, the tale of the meeting in Galilee. Instead we learn that the women fled from the tomb and said nothing to anyone because they were afraid. Then we are told nothing more.[3] As New Testament scholar Norman Petersen has said, the other shoe does not drop. The frustration of expectations is enormous.

Thus, readers have long worked to make sense of Mark's ending. The writer of Matthew gives us the "rest of the story," so to speak, by telling of a meeting in Galilee. So "the other shoe drops" in the conclusion of the first gospel. Other, later Markan readers were more bold. They actually wrote new endings for Mark's gospel, the so-called shorter and longer (vv. 9–16) endings that appear in most Bibles today.[4] Some contemporary biblical scholars have wondered if there was more to the original ending of Mark that has been lost. Other scholars have tried mightily to wrest some sense from the ending as it stands.

Literary critics could have told us that readers of Mark would do all these things. As Petersen noted, the end of a text turns out not to be the end of the work "when the narrator leaves unfinished business for the reader to complete, thoughtfully and imaginatively, not textually,"[5] as Mark obviously does. I am most persuaded by the efforts of New Testament scholars such as Alan Culpepper and Thomas Boomershine to complete the unfinished business of Mark. Boomershine argues that readers understand that the women's silence is wrong. Yet we sympathize and identify with them because we are told they were afraid—most of us know what it is like to be silent out of fear. The effect of this ending, according to Boomershine, is to appeal for repentance from the wrong response to the young man's words: "In the silences surrounding the climactic short statements of 16:8 and the surprising ending, Mark invites his audience to reflect on their own response to the dilemma which the women faced."[6] Similarly, Culpepper claims, "Mark was a skillful writer. Perhaps shock and surprise were the reactions he intended for the church to have, for now it knew everything the women knew. So, the question comes home to haunt those who hear Mark's gospel. How *could* they, how can *we*, hear these words, go, and tell no one?"[7]

My work with *good* stories has not suggested a new or better way to resolve the conundrum created by Mark's ending. I believe, however, that other *good* stories may help us read Mark's ending in such a way that we gain a clearer sense of the unfinished work Mark hoped we might complete.

We have given much attention in our work thus far to the "seeing" motif in Mark's story (as well as in other stories). Consequently, we cannot help but be drawn to the words of the young man at the tomb that Jesus has gone to Galilee, where disciples will *see* him.[8] Once our attention is there, however, we cannot stop, for we read on to see what the women will see. When we do, we encounter the women's fear and silence as they leave the tomb. Now we may think, "Ahh, fear again." We have found *seeing* and *fear* to be important aspects of Mark and the stories and also relevant to our living today. Now we find them coming together at the end of Mark's story. Given what we know from Mark and the stories about sight as insightfulness, about who sees and who does not and why, and about human fearfulness, we sense that there must be a connection between what the young man at the tomb calls the women to see and their fear and consequent silence. That connection forms the heart of this chapter.

So we will first consider the possibility of reading the young man's use of "see" as another Markan call to insightfulness. Second, we will see what light that reading sheds on the women's fear and silence. Third, we will consider how the insightfulness, fear, and silence drawn together at the end of Mark's story challenge us to finish the unfinished business of the gospel. In completing these tasks, we will find again that Mark touches the ragged edges of life, questions our neatly ordered worlds, and unveils our human condition as other *good* stories do. Finally, as I turn to issues of contemporary relevance, to ways Mark calls us to be more authentically human, I find myself compelled to end this study similarly to the way Mark ends this great story, that is, with questions rather than answers about what we are doing in response to this gospel we say we believe.

"There You Will See Him"

The last words of the young man to the women were, "He is going before you into Galilee; there you will see him, just as he said to you." Despite the women's ensuing silence, many readers have understood Mark's ending to point toward a meeting between the resurrected Jesus and his followers in Galilee. Petersen, for example, has argued that Mark's narrator has been so reliable throughout the gospel that readers can only understand 16:8 as highly ironic. So "even while the women are muddling about, as the disciples and the establishment had previously muddled about (Mark 14–15), Jesus, having risen, is on his way to Galilee where the disciples will soon see him."[9] Thus, says Petersen, 16:7 directs the reader's imagination to understand the meeting in Galilee as having happened and to bring closure to the narrative.[10] Others insist the ending points instead to the so-called "second coming" of Jesus that they believe Mark anticipated happening in Galilee.[11]

Both these perspectives, however, read the young man's words, "there you will *see* him," literally, as seeing done with physical eyes. What possibilities for new interpretations exist if we understand this use of "seeing" as the insightfulness we have found throughout Mark?

Galilee as Place and Symbol

We make a start toward answering this question when we understand that Galilee is both place and symbol for Mark. It is Jesus' home–we are introduced to him as coming from "Nazareth of Galilee" (1:9). It is also the place where he first went after his wilderness experience with the extraordinary announcement that "the *basileia* of God has drawn near" (1:14–15). He journeyed all over the region preaching and teaching, casting out evil, healing those who were suffering, and calling disciples. From Galilee Jesus ventured into foreign areas, where his followers witnessed his breakdown of political, social, and theological barriers. So Galilee is the place of mission on behalf of God's activity in the world. Now, at 16:7 his followers are told they must return to Galilee to begin their lives anew. Therefore, Galilee, as it brings to mind Jesus' journey through that region and from there to foreign areas, all the while preaching and showing the *basileia* of God to have drawn near, becomes Mark's symbol of the mission of Jesus' followers after the events in Jerusalem.[12]

And the resurrected Jesus is going to Galilee ahead of them. As *good* stories go, this news is not surprising. In quest stories the hero must venture beyond the known and familiar place into the darkness if she or he will accomplish the goal of the quest. Then the hero must come back from that yonder place and return home with the Golden Fleece or the wisdom gained to renew the community, the nation, the planet, or whatever.[13] Similarly, in pilgrimage stories the seeker journeys to a holy place in order to return and bring wisdom and healing to those back home.[14] So the youngest son in "The Golden Bird" must return to his father's castle after gaining the golden bird (not to mention the golden horse and the princess) to expose the treachery of his brothers and free the princess' brother from the spell that has turned him into a fox.

Eastern Europeans have long told tales of the young girl Vasalisa the wise. In one of them her dying mother gave Vasalisa a doll (which looked like Vasalisa). The doll was a "mother's blessing" to guide her should she ever lose her way. After mourning the mother's death, Vasalisa's father married a woman with two daughters who secretly hated Vasalisa. The three of them conspired to send Vasalisa to get fire from Baba Yaga, the witch, who would surely eat her. So began Vasalisa's journey through the dark forest. Guided by her doll, she found Baba Yaga's strange house and encountered the fearsome creature herself. With her doll's help she completed the tasks the Baba Yaga gave her and answered the questions she was asked so that the hag finally gave her fire. Then, with newfound confidence and strength, Vasalisa returned with the fire and rid her home and family of her stepmother and stepsisters.[15]

The hobbit Bilbo Baggins was called to join a company of dwarves seeking to drive the dragon Smaug from the dwarves' ancestral home (where the dwarves' gold remained). Along the journey he found the One Ring, which, in the hands of the great sorcerer Sauron, would put all of Middle-earth under the power of evil. When their quest ended successfully, Bilbo and the wizard Gandalf turned back toward the Shire. They traveled until they came to land as familiar to Bilbo as his own hands and toes. "Coming to a rise, he could see his own Hill in the distance, and he stopped suddenly and said:

> 'Roads go ever ever on
> Under cloud and under star,
> Yet feet that wandering have gone
> Turn at last to home afar.
> Eyes that fire and sword have seen
> And horror in the halls of stone
> Look at last on meadows green
> And trees and hills they long have known.'

"Gandalf looked at him. 'My dear Bilbo!' he said. 'Something is the matter with you! You are not the hobbit that you were.'"[16] T. S. Eliot, another twentieth-century poet (and a nonfictional one!) echoes Bilbo's sentiment in notable lines from his famous poem *Four Quartets:*

> We shall not cease from exploration
> And the end of all our exploring
> Will be to arrive where we started
> And know the place for the first time.[17]

Theologian Dorothee Soelle believes the stories (and Eliot's poem as well) are telling us something deeply true. Without the return home, she says, the spiritual journey "becomes nothing but a means to the end of private comfort and self-protection." But as we have seen throughout our study of Mark and the stories, self-centeredness is never the goal of the spiritual journey. To the contrary, when we follow Christ and persevere to the end, we journey to the emptying and surrendering of the ego and discover our true selves, that is, our deepest self-confirmation. Then we travel back into and for the world. According to Soelle, this return journey home to share what we have gained is indispensable. Being authentically human calls forth from us love of God *and* love of neighbor.[18] Becoming whole requires us to turn both inward and outward. From this perspective, therefore, it is no surprise that Jesus is returning home to Galilee. He is not content with his personal vindication. His mission and journey continue. Beyond his own resurrection the folks "back home" still need to experience the nearness of God's *basileia*. So if his disciples follow him to Galilee, they will *see* him because that is where he is journeying now.

"Seeing" Jesus in Galilee

Now we can give our attention to what Jesus' disciples are called to see. If we focus on Galilee as symbolic of the return journey of Jesus and of the mission of those who follow Jesus after the events of Jerusalem, perhaps we should be encouraged not to look for a specific event such as a resurrection appearance or the "second coming." Such would be an incident that happens in a geographical place, both of which (incident and place) we see with our physical eyes. Perhaps instead we are being invited by the young man to *see* that Jesus has been raised and is on the way to "Galilee" with all that that means.

Responding to such an invitation requires great insightfulness, though we may not realize this at first. My experiences with church folks suggest that many of us have feeble theologies of the resurrection. As one of my students put it, we often imagine that on Easter morning Jesus woke up, stretched and yawned, peeled off the grave clothes as we would pajamas, pushed back the stone, and walked out much the same as he was before. That view, however, is much closer to the concept of resuscitation than to the New Testament proclamation that Jesus was resurrected. We need to *see* the difference between resurrection and resuscitation. Specifically, for our purposes, we need to see what Mark may have meant by "He has been raised; he is not here" (16:6).

Mark actually offers us little with which to judge his understanding of Jesus' resurrection. Following each of his three predictions of his own death Jesus states without elaboration that he will be raised on the third day (8:31; 9:31; 10:34). Mark records that while coming down from the mountain on which the transfiguration took place, Jesus orders his followers to tell no one about the vision until after he has risen from the dead (9:9). Finally, for Mark, Jesus affirms his belief in resurrection in his argument with the Sadducees over the hypothetical woman who was married seven times (12:26). These are the only explicit references to resurrection in the gospel outside chapter 16. From even these scant references, however, glimmers of Mark's understanding of Jesus' resurrection can be discerned. These glimmers in turn give strong hints about what Mark wanted followers to "see" in "Galilee."

Jesus' Resurrection According to Mark

Careful scrutiny of Mark's gospel presents us with three major considerations to weigh. We can first note briefly that Mark's gospel is considered by many scholars to be an apocalyptic gospel that originated in what can be called an apocalyptic community. Biblical scholar Howard Clark Kee, for example, describes the Markan community as an apocalyptic community in the tradition of Jewish groups that considered themselves heirs to the prophetic promises concerning the new covenant.[19] New Testament scholar Brian Blount believes Mark viewed his people as "present pockets of transformative resistance" that represent even now the future reality of the *basileia* of God, which will come in fullness.[20] As we have noted several times, Jesus in Mark declares that the *basileia* of God has drawn near. Mark believed that God was already at work transforming their world and that followers of Jesus join themselves to this work of God.

A second consideration is to note that three of Mark's five references to Jesus' resurrection appear in apocalyptic contexts (the other two conclude without elaboration Jesus' last passion predictions). For example, the first of Jesus' predictions of his own resurrection in 8:31 is followed shortly thereafter by his call to disciples to take up their crosses and follow him (8:34). To "take up the cross" in Mark's context was an invitation to accept the risks, including martyrdom, of challenging the current and unjust power structures in the world.[21] How can anyone find the courage to receive an invitation like that? By believing that there is life in God that transcends one's current existence. So losing one's life for the sake of Jesus and the gospel is actually to gain Life (8:35) when Jesus comes in the (apocalyptic) glory of God with the holy angels (8:38). The remaining two references are the conversation between Jesus and his disciples following the transfiguration experience (9:9–13), and that between Jesus and the Sadducees regarding whose wife a seven times–married woman would be in the resurrection (12:18–27). Both these stories also link apocalyptic hopes and resurrection.[22]

Our third consideration in our search for Mark's understanding of Jesus' resurrection is that we should not be surprised that Mark associated resurrection with the age to come, for other apocalyptic thinkers did so as well. Indeed, it appears that explicit Jewish reflections on resurrection occurred when Jewish apocalyptic thinking first flourished during Antiochus Epiphanes' reign of terror over Israel in the early second century B.C.E. Biblical scholar N. T. Wright's review of the apocalypses of this period is helpful for our efforts to understand Mark's view of Jesus' resurrection. Wright concluded that these apocalyptic Jews were not looking for an end to the space-time world in which we live. Were they looking for an end to the present world order that oppressed and persecuted God's faithful people? Yes, Wright claims, but not an end to the space-time world. Instead, Jews hoped for a renewal of the world and all that was associated with that: forgiveness of sins, the reestablishment of Israel as the true people of the covenant God, and the renewal of creation.

Resurrection in this context is a divine reward for martyrs. Given God's justice and mercy, it was inconceivable that those who died in the struggle to bring the new world into being should be left out of the blessing when it finally came. But resurrection is also much more than a reward, for, in this context, resurrection and renewal go hand in hand.[23] Thus, when viewed from this vantage point, the possibilities for interpreting resurrection language widen dramatically. Far more than simply new life for dead people, resurrection also becomes a metaphor, a literary means of expressing a historical, social, and political hope for transformation and renewal.[24] It signals that God is bringing into being the new age, which is characterized by the end of oppression and suffering in favor of God's justice and mercy. Indeed, Wright claims that in the early days of Christianity the powers that be worried greatly about announcements of Jesus' resurrection precisely because of the radical transformations such announcements implied (cf. Acts 4:1–3).[25]

These careful considerations–(1) that Mark was an apocalyptic gospel from an apocalyptic community, (2) that resurrection and apocalyptic thinking are linked in the gospel, and (3) that Mark, in this regard, was like apocalyptic Jews whose reflections on resurrection occurred in the midst of their apocalyptic hope for the renewal of the world–now weighed together allow for the following suggestions regarding Mark's understanding of Jesus' resurrection. If, for Mark, resurrection is an apocalyptic event that happens at the end of the present age and the start of the age to come, *and* Jesus is resurrected, *then* the present age is already passing away and the new age has begun. Jesus' proclamation that the *basileia* of God has drawn near is, therefore, dramatically confirmed! Jesus' resurrection illustrates for us that nothing will ever be the same as it was before, for the apocalyptic renewal of the world is underway.[26] Consequently, if we understand *see* in Mark 16:7 to mean "insightfulness," then followers of Jesus who go to Galilee, the symbol of Jesus' mission of announcing the present reality of God's *basileia,* will *see* that Jesus is resurrected. They will *see*, that is, that the new age has begun, that God is indeed at work transforming their world. Therefore, by means of his resurrection, Jesus' followers are being given an opportunity to see what they had not seen before!

Enormous Implications!

The implications of the proclamation that Jesus has been raised, therefore, are huge. Followers of the risen Jesus will share in God's transformation of the world when they make the return journey to Galilee, *see* that Jesus is raised, and take up Jesus' mission of announcing that God is making God's *basileia* a reality in our midst.

Throughout the gospel, Mark has helped us see what this mission involves. The *basileia* of God becomes a reality when followers of Jesus form an inclusive community that welcomes men, women, and children; Jews and gentiles; lepers; tax collectors and other sinners; blind beggars; Syrophoenician women; scribes; centurions; and anybody else who wishes to be accepted. There should be no structures of domination or exploitation within the community. Instead members align themselves with the least ones (9:36–37) and practice service (10:43b–45), forgiveness (11:25), and prayer for God's will to be done and the present evil order to be undone (9:28–29, 11:12–24). The feeding stories suggest people's needs will be met in this community. The healing stories and exorcisms suggest individuals will be set free from whatever binds them and will find wholeness among God's people. By devoting themselves (note 3:35) to such liberating and compassionate expressions of God's justice and mercy, disciples of Jesus place themselves now in the age to come and experience the renewal of the world God is bringing about. If they go to Galilee, if they join themselves to Jesus' mission, in other words, if they make his journey their journey, they will *see* that he is resurrected and all that means for them and the world.

They Said Nothing to Anyone, for They Were Afraid

So what do the women do with this good news that Jesus is resurrected and the young man's call to go to Galilee and *see* him? They run from the tomb and tell no one, because they are afraid. Here is the shocking ending of Mark that has so confounded Mark's readers: The young man's good news is met by the women's fear and silence. What is going on here? Of what are the women so afraid that they become totally silent (the Greek is emphatic)? Well, the story ends here, so Mark does not answer this question directly. We can only look in the story for clues about their fear.

Fear of Persecution

Would the women have been afraid of persecution and suffering? Probably. Clearly, if Jesus lived as though God's *basileia* had drawn near and suffered for doing so, the odds were good that the same fate awaited his followers. In fact, Jesus said as much. "Take up your crosses," he called to disciples (8:34), inviting them to accept the risks of confronting the earthly powers with God's transformation of the world. Countless examples from history tell us that earthly powers are not fond of people with such messages. Another time Jesus told followers that those who give up house, family, and land for the gospel will receive a hundredfold in family members, houses, and lands *with persecutions* (10:29–30). During the apocalyptic discourse, Jesus warned followers, "They will hand you over to the councils; and you will be beaten in the synagogues; and you will stand before governors and kings for my sake to bear witness to them" (13:9). Now the risen Jesus was going to Galilee to continue the mission that got him killed, and he was beckoning them to follow.

And yet, precisely because Jesus' life and words so plainly indicate persecution to be a real possibility, I am unconvinced that such suffering accounts primarily for the women's fear in 16:8. After all, they would have been living with the possibility of persecution for some time. Indeed, these women had faced this threat already. Even after the other disciples fled from Gethsemane (14:50) and Peter denied Jesus (14:66–72), apparently out of fear of persecution, the women were still present. They witnessed Jesus' death (15:40–41) and burial (15:47) and went to the tomb to anoint him when the sabbath had passed (16:1). Consequently, I am hard pressed to accept that Mark wanted us to believe that the young man's happy words suddenly made the women so fearful of persecution that they ran away in silence when they had not been so afraid before. I believe we should look elsewhere for help in more fully understanding the women's fear in 16:8.

Remembering Another Fear

As we have seen, this story is not the first in Mark's gospel where the response to an extraordinary happening is fear. We remember the disciples' fear after Jesus stilled the storm (4:41), the fear of the Gerasene people who found the crazed demoniac restored to his right mind by Jesus' word (5:15–17), and the hemorrhaging woman who feared and trembled because she knew she had been healed (5:33). Then there are the *good* stories, such as that of Rat and Mole, who loved the Friend and Helper but also feared him. Or the story of Frodo's friends at the beginning of this chapter, who encountered Gandalf alive again after they thought he was lost to them forever. In that moment they stood "between wonder, joy, and fear...and found no words to say." In the last chapter we saw that such fear in the presence of the Wholly Other is part of the human condition, because we saw what our affirmation that God is light and truth means. Experiencing God's presence necessarily exposes the ragged edges of our lives and shows the ways that our neatly ordered worlds are not so neat and not so orderly.

We can return to the text at hand, therefore, and ask if the women's fear in Mark 16:8 was the result of just such an extraordinary sense of God's presence, which was evoked by the young man's words. Might they have simply not believed Jesus when he announced that the *basileia* of God had drawn near? If so, then the young man's announcement that "Jesus has been raised" would have made them aware, really for the first time, how near to them God had drawn and was at work. Might they then have had some sense that this encounter with God had huge implications for the ragged edges of their lives and their neatly ordered worlds? It surely seems possible.

Then, if we consider this possibility, we must wonder what this divine encounter threatens to expose about the women in Mark's story. What transformation would going to Galilee and *seeing* that Jesus is raised call forth that causes them to run away in total silence? Therein lies the problem, of course. As we saw in chapter 4, their fear is very human and natural, even unavoidable. But their flight and silence in response to their fear startle us. Again, Mark's story does not answer our question directly. Again, we can only look for clues in the gospel to help us.

The clues this time are more vague. There are few references to the women to help us understand them well. On the one hand, Mark 15:40–41 indicates that the women were part of a large group of disciples who surrounded Jesus from the early days of his work in Galilee and who journeyed with him to Jerusalem. As we noted earlier, this group included but was not limited to the Twelve (see 4:10). So the women's participation in this group of disciples hints at close ties between themselves and the Twelve.

On the other hand, the women distinguished themselves from the Twelve by their being present at the crucifixion (though from afar), burial, and tomb. In so doing they risked persecution in ways the others did not. Thus, their presence at the last events of Jesus' life suggests at first that they were not like the Twelve, whose real allegiance lay with themselves rather than with God, as we discussed in chapter 3.

But then the women's flight and silence must cause us to wonder. Had they, in fact, not seen any more clearly than the Twelve the radical new order and renewal of the world that God was bringing about as Jesus proclaimed? Like the Twelve, did their allegiance rest ultimately in themselves? Did they hope for their group to claim the top spots in a still hierarchically organized world? If this is the case, then they too would have been disinclined to see that God was at work to end all structures in which some people have power over others. Had they thus become as blind to Jesus as the Twelve? If this is the case, then the women would have gone to the tomb that morning only to anoint Jesus' body and grieve his death. If this is the case, the young man's news at the tomb that Jesus was resurrected and his call to them to go to Galilee and *see* Jesus would expose their blindness to the nearness of God's *basileia*. The young man's news would expose where their allegiance actually lay.

Probably most of us have thought of Jesus' resurrection as unambiguously good news. We love that the "good guy wins," that life is stronger than death, that Jesus is alive and well. We love Jesus' resurrection for Jesus' sake. But the women's fear, flight, and silence suggest a flip side to consider. Parker Palmer maintains that death in its various forms can actually be comforting. Resurrection and new life, on the other hand, are demanding and frightening. For example, going to war, with all the death it brings, is easier than struggling to understand ourselves and our enemies, or to communicate with the enemies, or to feel compassion for them. Or we accept the notion that there are "acceptable levels of death" from such things as carcinogenic chemicals and nuclear power plants because otherwise we might have to change our way of life.[27]

Along these lines, consider an apocryphal story of Peter that has him encountering a blind beggar beside the road. Moved with compassion, Peter healed the man. But the man leapt to his feet enraged. He screamed at Peter, "You fool! You have destroyed my way of making a living!" Then in one swift, violent act he gouged out his own eyes and collapsed back into the street.[28] A close friend from my seminary days lived a story with similarities to this one. While struggling with depression, she was assigned to preach the story of the paralyzed man by the pool of Beth-zatha (John 5:1–47). She told me that her reflections on the text had made her aware of the choices between "life and death" that she faced. She said, "While I am depressed, you are especially kind to me. You take care of me and don't expect anything from me. In many ways life is easier. So Jesus' question to this man has become the key question in my life right now—do I want to be healed?"

Poet Julia Esquivel, no stranger to injustice, suffering, and death in her native Guatemala, also knows of this "flip side" to news about resurrection:

It isn't the noise in the streets
that keeps us from resting, my friend,
nor is it the shouts of the young people
coming out drunk from the "St. Pauli,"
nor is it the tumult of those who pass by excitedly
on their way to the mountains.
It is something within us that doesn't let us sleep,

that doesn't let us rest,
that won't stop pounding
deep inside,…
What keeps us from sleeping
is that they have threatened us with Resurrection![29]

Have the women in Mark encountered this flip side to the story? Are they threatened with resurrection? Just think of the advantages for them if Jesus stayed dead. Any hatred they felt toward the religious leaders in the temple or Roman officials would be justified, since those people killed someone they loved. The same would be true of any vengeance they might plot. Or they could understandably think, "Nothing ever changes anyway, so why bother?" and just go home to resume the lives they'd led before Jesus. They could even be forgiven for giving in to despair. Jesus' death had no doubt been difficult enough to cope with. How much easier now if he just stayed dead rather than being resurrected, journeying home to Galilee, and calling them to follow!

For if he is resurrected, God is indeed at work drawing the *basileia* very near. God is working to transform the world. Nothing will ever be the same! If Jesus is resurrected, then their willingness to be part of something larger than themselves, part of what God is doing in the world, is being tested. If they are not so willing, the young man's news will expose this ragged edge of their lives. So are the women threatened with resurrection? It seems quite possible, and this could be a reason for their flight and silence. They run and say nothing so as to remain unexposed, to avoid the challenges of transformation, to keep their neatly ordered world intact. It appears that the insightfulness to which they were called has threatened them so that they are scared speechless.

At the end, I find that I can only ask if I have understood well the women's flight and silence. I can only wonder if they might have feared this kind of exposure and transformation from an extraordinary encounter with God, if they were threatened with resurrection. Mark does not tell us these things explicitly. So we are left with our questions. But maybe that's a good thing for us.

Ending the Story

As we noted earlier in this chapter, the end of a text is not the end of the work when the storyteller leaves unfinished business for the audience to complete. Left with our questions, we clearly have unfinished business with Mark. The story is not yet ended. We have work to do.

Since Mark gives us no more information, the only way I know to finish our business is to put ourselves in the women's sandals, as a number of scholars have suggested, and ask: If I had been there, if *we* had been there, then what? If we had seen the young man dressed in white and heard his words, "Jesus has been raised! Go to Galilee! There you will *see* him."...If we had had this kind of encounter with that which is Holy so that we were more acutely aware of how near us God has drawn and what God is doing in our world...If we were afraid that this encounter with God, who is light, truth, and consuming fire, would expose the ragged edges of our lives, subvert our neatly ordered worlds, and call us to transformation...If we were called to *see* that Jesus is resurrected...If we were summoned to make his journey our journey, then what would *we* do?

What Should We Do?

One way to clarify our answers for ourselves is first to ask the question, What *should* we do? We ought actually to have a fairly good sense of the answer to this question as a result of lessons learned in the last chapter. But now, other *good* stories reinforce what we have already seen and show us how we might end Mark's story.

The hobbits Frodo and Sam were journeying to the Mountain of Fire in the center of the evil lord Sauron's kingdom. They were on a desperate quest to destroy the One Ring before Sauron got it for himself and destroyed everything. Frodo was exhausted from the burden of having been entrusted with the quest. But Sam got him up and moving again quickly after each rest lest fear completely overtake them and they give up. One morning before waking Frodo, however, Sam gazed at the mountain, still fifty miles away, and

> As he worked things out, slowly a new dark thought grew in his mind. Never for long had hope died in his staunch heart, and always until now he had taken some thought for their return. But the bitter truth came home to him at last: at best their provision would take them to their goal; and when their task was done, there they would come to an end, alone, houseless, foodless in the midst of a terrible desert. There could be no return.
>
> "So that was the job I felt I had to do when I started," thought Sam: "to help Mr. Frodo to the last step and then die with him? Well, if that is the job then I must do it."

But even as hope died in Sam, or seemed to die, it was turned to new strength.[30]

In Frances Hodgson Burnett's *The Secret Garden* the young orphan Mary is sent to live with her uncle in a great mansion in Yorkshire. She is befriended by Dickon, the brother of one of the servants. She has started enjoying her new life when she stumbles onto a cousin her own age living in the mansion as well. Colin also did not know about Mary. "Did no one tell you I had come to live here?" Mary asks Colin. "No, they daren't. I should have been afraid you would see me. I am like this always, ill and having to lie down…If I live I may be a hunchback, but I shan't live." Later Mary tells Dickon, "Colin is so afraid of [becoming a hunchback like his father] himself that he won't sit up." She takes Dickon to meet Colin. The two of them tell him about the "secret garden" they have discovered and plot to get Colin out to see it. On the day they succeed in doing so, Colin watches them work among the plants and flowers and declares:

> "I'm going to see everything grow here. I'm going to grow here myself."
>
> "That tha' will," said Dickon. "Us'll have thee walkin' about here an' diggin' same as other folk afore long."
>
> "Walk!" said Colin. "Dig! Shall I?"
>
> "For sure tha' will. Tha's got legs o' thine own, same as other folks!"
>
> "Nothing really ails them," said Colin, "but they are so thin and weak. They shake so that I'm afraid to try to stand on them."
>
> "When tha' stops being afraid tha'lt stand on them," Dickon said.[31]

The Native American story of Jumping Mouse was a significant help to us in the last chapter, and it helps us here again. Like the little mouse, Colin was always afraid–of Mary seeing him, of becoming a hunchback, of his shaky legs, of dying. But we remember how Jumping Mouse did not allow his fears to dominate him. He continued his journey even when he was afraid. There is a telling moment early in the story when the little mouse's searching led him to the river. There he met the wise old frog who asked him if he would like to have some "medicine power."

> "Medicine power? Me?" asked Little Mouse. "Yes, yes! If it is possible."

"Then crouch as low as you can, and then jump as high as you are able! You will have your medicine!" Frog said.

Little Mouse did as he was instructed. He crouched as low as he could and jumped. And when he did, his eyes saw the Sacred Mountains.

Little Mouse could hardly believe his eyes. But there they were! But then he fell back to earth, and he landed in the river!

Little Mouse became frightened and scrambled back to the bank. He was wet and frightened nearly to death.

"You have tricked me," Little Mouse screamed at the frog.

"Wait," said the frog. "You are not harmed. Do not let your fear and anger blind you. What did you see?"

"I," Mouse stammered, "I, I saw the Sacred Mountains!"[32]

The frog's wisdom is what Dickon shares with Colin. When Colin stops "being" afraid, when he stops allowing his fears to blind him and to determine how he will live his life, then he will stand up. Colin does, indeed, cease being dominated by his fears and dreams of the day he can announce to his absent father, "I am quite well and I shall live to be a man."[33] And Sam, having faced his fear of death, finds new strength to lead Frodo to the completion of their quest. They even have their longed-for journey home. And Little Mouse sees through his fear and anger to the Sacred Mountains. These stories reiterate what we saw in chapter 4. All the heroes journeyed forward by facing what they feared rather than running away, by choosing not to allow their fears to determine their way.

With the impact of these stories reverberating in our heads, let us return to our unfinished business with Mark's story. If we had seen the young man dressed in white and heard him say: "Jesus has been raised! Go to Galilee! There you will *see* him."...If we are called to *see* that Jesus is resurrected and all that that means for us and for the world...If we had had such an extraordinary encounter with the Holy...If we are afraid that this encounter with God is exposing where our allegiances really lie...If we are being summoned in this way by God, then what should we do? The *good* stories tell us we should *not* run and be silent! They tell us that instead we should face that which we fear. They tell us we should accept the exposure of the ragged edges of our lives and the subversion of our neatly ordered worlds. Then we can be transformed into those who share in God's *basileia,* which has drawn near us.

To "write" a good ending to Mark's *good* story, therefore, we should go to Galilee. That is, we should embark on the mission, begin the journey of the followers of Jesus. We should *see* that Jesus is resurrected. Nothing will ever be the same as it was before, for God has drawn near and is renewing creation. We should *see* what this insight means for us. In light of what Mark has told us about God's work in the world to usher in the *basileia,* we should ask ourselves, for example, if we are resisting our culture's emphasis on appearance. Or we should ask if we are resisting calls to consume more and more, which impoverishes others and destroys the Earth's beauty. Or we should ask if we are resisting the seduction of power. We should *see* if this insight regarding Jesus' resurrection exposes ways we have not been resistant to these temptations because our allegiance has been ultimately to self rather than to God. We should *see* if we have been hiding our allegiance to self behind our religious service. We should *see* whether or not we have become our fears.

We will fear this exposure—it is hard to see ourselves in God's light and truth. But when we have seen ourselves, we can receive what we see and open ourselves to God's transforming work. We can let go of our ego-centeredness and commit ourselves wholly to God. When we have done so, we need no longer think of others as "those people" whom we must be better than, for we will be able to *see* the image of God imprinted into all of us. Then we can *see* God's presence in our midst in the most unexpected people and circumstances and join ourselves to God's efforts to draw us all together into the discipleship of equals. Then we can *see* how many ways we can place ourselves already in the age to come and live now in the freedom and compassion of God. To do so, according to the stories, is joyous! But doing so is also frightening, for we risk confrontation with the earthly powers. Thus, to do so is to jeopardize our own privilege, positions, and ambitions. To do so, according to the stories, is to share in God's renewal of our world. To do so is to continue the journey to which God has called us. To do so is to come home to ourselves and give our hearts a chance to laugh.

What Will We Do?

Ah, but *good* stories are, as John Shea said, "wagers on the wind." They speak their truth and are over. They only show us what is possible. They cannot tell us what we are doing or what we will do.

They cannot tell us how we are finishing the unfinished business of Mark's story. At the end—which is where we are—we can only tell that story ourselves with our lives.

Concluding Thoughts

Mark's story ought to end happily. Jesus has been raised! Death is not stronger than life! Jesus' proclamation that the *basileia* of God has drawn near is dramatically confirmed by his resurrection! The women disciples who journeyed to the tomb are given this good news and told to make the return journey to Galilee. There they will *see* Jesus, just as he promised them.

Instead the story ends jarringly. We are told the women said not one thing to anyone, for they were afraid. Then we are told nothing more. We are left with sputtered questions. How could they? Of what are they so afraid that they are utterly silent? What do we expect from them instead?

Then, when we probe the gospel for answers to our questions, we uncover the "flip side" to the good news of the resurrection, the threat that resurrection is to our neatly ordered worlds. For if we *see* that Jesus is resurrected, we will see that God is bringing the *basileia* near us. The age to come has begun. God's transformation of the world is under way. But what if we have invested ourselves in gaining wealth, power, and status in the world as it is and have refused to see how our pursuits may have hurt others or the Earth? What if we have pledged ultimate allegiance to ourselves rather than to God? What if we have hidden where our allegiance really lies behind our religious service? What if we have hidden this reality even from ourselves? Then the insight to which we are called, the nearness of God, and the transformation that the Holy One is bringing about will expose us—are we willing to face such exposure?

So if we were in the women's shoes, what would we do? We would be afraid. There is no way for us who are human to avoid being afraid of exposure in the light and truth of God. So while we are afraid, as the women were afraid, what will we do?

There Mark's story leaves us, for the answers to these questions cannot be given on the pages of the gospel. These answers are within us.

CONCLUSION

The Power of *This* Story

So *good* stories are powerful. They touch a deep, spiritual place in our lives, reminding us who we are and from whence we have come. They help us along our way to remember what it means to be authentically human. Many of these *good* stories may be called *sacred* stories as they heed the Presence of God that hides in every breath, word, sound, and silence. In so doing they offer us a sense of resolution and truth. They also relate our failures, lacks, and losses, thus unsettling us by making us face the ragged edges of our lives. But then they sustain us with illumination and heal us. And so, *good* stories call us to come home to ourselves.

Mark's gospel is just such a *good* story for us.

At its beginning Mark paints Jesus' story with the colors of a journey story. Thus, the gospel points us to the ancient wisdom that sees life as a spiritual journey. The story begins with a disturbing, disrupting moment in its world—John the Baptist calls the people to repent, to go a new way, and promises that a Stronger One is coming. Then Jesus is summoned to the Way of the Lord at his baptism. He sees the heavens ripped open and the Spirit descending on him. So God is on the loose in our world. Something new and disrupting is indeed being unleashed!

The Spirit then empowers Jesus for the journey to which he has been called and immediately drives him into the wilderness to face Satan. In the language of journey stories, this is Jesus' first threshold, that is, his first awareness that the journey to which he has been called will not be easy. So he is tempted there to quit the journey. He does not. Instead, he leaves the wilderness announcing a new hope: The *basileia* of God has drawn near!

Jesus then journeys all over Galilee and beyond proclaiming this good news and demonstrating what it means. As he teaches in parables, touches lepers, includes tax collectors and fishermen among his disciples, forgives sin, feeds hungry people, drives demons away,

111

heals and praises women and Gentiles, and insists that holiness is a matter of one's heart, he shows that God is at work in the world transforming the way people relate to one another and to God.

And he arouses opposition. Those invested in the world as it is do not see the transformation he proclaims in God's name, or they see it and reject it. So the way Jesus journeys is a road of trials. It leads him to Jerusalem, to his "dark night of the soul" in Gethsemane where he chooses God's will over his own, and to ultimate self-denial at the cross.

But he is resurrected! This apocalyptic event means the present age is passing away and the new age has already begun. Thus, the presence of the *basileia* of God is dramatically confirmed. God is indeed on the loose in our world, and nothing will ever be the same.

Now Jesus is making the return journey to Galilee. His followers are told to go there and *see* him. Here Mark's story ends, with only the sense that Mark's readers are being summoned to join Jesus on his journey along the Way of the Lord.

If we wish to follow him, we must *see*. One spiritual teacher says seeing is the key discipline for the spiritual journey. Another says we do not naturally see and have to be taught. Mark's harping on this theme suggests our storyteller would agree. To become authentically human as God intends, we must see what we hear! We must see evil's deceptions. We must see ourselves. We must see that the *basileia* of God has drawn near. We must be aware, perceptive, and insightful, for all that we see (with our physical eyes) is not what it seems. We must look beneath surfaces and beyond the moment to the implications, consequences, and possibilities of our words and deeds. We must see that the way Jesus goes–into the wilderness, through Galilee, to Jerusalem, to Gethsemane, to the cross, and back to Galilee–is the Way of the Lord, the way to Paradise, the way to come home to ourselves.

So much in our culture, however, exhorts us to sleepwalk rather than see. We are encouraged to focus on appearances and possessions–external things we see with our physical eyes–as the means of evaluating ourselves and others. We are encouraged *not to see* how our consumption is destroying the Earth, how harmful the emphasis on appearance is to adolescent girls, or the myriad signs telling us our consumer culture is not satisfying our deepest longings. Instead we are told we only need more and bigger and newer (things and appearances).

Such an outlook not only does not satisfy our deepest longings. It also fosters and nurtures ego-centeredness, which is contrary to the spiritual journey. Traveling the Way of the Lord requires of us self-denial instead. We must journey to the emptying of our egocentricity if we wish to discover the deepest self-confirmation, or what many spiritual teachers call our true selves. Consequently, the more we are invested in our egos, the more blind we will be to the way of self-denial to which God is calling us. Or maybe we will see it, but we will reject that way as God's way because it does not fit our image of God. One of the most challenging portraits Mark paints is of those who have found a sense of a God who serves them well, who grants them privileges and makes them powerful. Then they invest themselves in proclaiming this God and thus appear to be the most religious of people. In reality, their religious practice is a cover for their ego-centeredness. So if God should happen to be experienced outside their religious practices and understandings, they either cannot see God or they see but reject what they see because it does not serve them as they wish.

Consequently, "outsiders" to the religious structures are often the ones who have profound experiences of God. And "insiders" fear them. The insiders prefer to believe that their views of the world, truth, and God are the only ones, for often they have invested their very sense of self in these views. When they can be sure their views are the only ones, they can be comfortable in their "rightness." No wonder they like harmonious anthills in which there are no dissenting voices. No wonder the views of those who would be labeled as "other" feel like huge threats to them.

When religious insiders are ego-centered and have invested their sense of self in their religious beliefs, practices, and images of God that serve them well, their fear of the "other" will prevail in the decisions they make about these others. When that happens, evil is done. Mark's religious leaders feared Jesus because of his impact on the crowd, and they killed him. The Grand Inquisitor sent him away. Black people were not welcomed into white churches (and sometimes still aren't). Women who experienced a call from God to preach were called sinners and heretics and worse (and sometimes still are).

When religious insiders are ego-centered, their fear of God's near presence causes them to retreat from that presence. Make no mistake—all human beings will be afraid when they experience the divine presence. God's Light and Truth expose all of us and call all of us to change, to be transformed. Such change is a fearsome prospect. But for those who have invested themselves in their view of the world and their place in that world, such transformation brings great upheaval and thus seems overwhelmingly fearful. So they retreat from mystery to mastery and turn back to the world they control. And evil is done. They turn away those who bring the Divine Presence too near them. As the Gerasene people turned Jesus away. As many in the church today turn away gay and lesbian people who want to share the experiences of God they have had.

But we do not have to be dominated by our fears. If only we believe, if only we commit our way to the Way of the Lord, if only we pledge our allegiance to God rather than to self, we can journey forward even while we are afraid. And we *will* be afraid–all the spiritual teachers tell us this. Letting go of comfortable images of God or the world is scary. Seeing ourselves in the Light of God is scary. But we do not have to be dominated and blinded by our fears. We can be afraid *and* deny self *and* choose God's will over our own. We can be afraid *and* trust that the journey is taking us to the deepest self-confirmation, even when we feel as though we are surely losing ourselves. We can be afraid *and* believe that the transformation and renewal God is bringing about within us and among us is the way to be authentically human. We can be afraid *and* receive the *basileia* of God as children. As did the hemorrhaging woman who feared and trembled *and* came forward to Jesus. As did Scrooge, who welcomed the spirit he feared most *and* become another man than what he'd been–and his heart laughed to see it.

But we are not finished when our hearts finally laugh. At this point we must make the journey back home, back into the world, to share the wisdom we have learned from traveling the Way of the Lord. We return, announcing that the *basileia* of God has indeed drawn near and showing how we may live in its reality now. We return home to show others how they may come home to themselves.

So the spiritual journey is not an easy way. All the stories tell us this. But maybe no story tells us as forcefully as Mark does. There Jesus journeys all the way to Golgotha. Mark's account of Jesus' death is stark and unrelieved by anything, such as the presence of his mother or of one of the victims' asking Jesus to remember him when Jesus comes into his kingdom. We are only told of Jesus' scream out of the darkness, "My God, my God, why have you forsaken me?" And God does not answer. Yet the next we hear of him, Jesus is risen and on his way to Galilee, on his way home. The spiritual journey is not an easy way, Mark tells us emphatically, but it *is* the way home. So if we journey to Galilee, we will *see* him.

Many times during the writing of this book I have thought of theologian Edward Farley's October 1997 lecture at Memphis Theological Seminary, in which he defined authentic faith as the worship of God because God is God. Worshiping God for any other reason—such as to get to heaven, to relieve stress, to find peace of mind—amounts to narcissistic (self-centered) religion, because our focus is really on ourselves rather than God.[1] His lecture caused me to think of the ways churches have typically "marketed" themselves. In my experience churches have said, "You really ought to come to our church because you can find peace, stress relief, and the comfort of knowing you are going to heaven." In other words, we have appealed to people's ego-centeredness to encourage them to join our churches!

Furthermore, if we define success in church as increasing the number of people present, then we had better "market" church in this way. We've already noted how much this culture is about pumping up ego. People are accustomed, therefore, to marketing strategies that stroke their egos. Many people expect and look for such. In addition, as Dorothee Soelle, among others, has observed, utopia is defined in our culture as the absence of suffering and getting through life without experiencing pain.[2] When we put these things together, we can hardly be surprised that many of us have not heard much in church about wilderness experiences, dark nights of the soul, or journeying to the emptying of our egos. Sermons such as that will not likely pack the pews in the ethos of our time. As one of my students suggested in a class studying Mark's gospel, we would not have any trouble today finding a seat in a "Markan church," for it would be a church that should be named something like "The Church of the Persecuted and Suffering Followers of Jesus."

But where have our ego-centeredness and desire for ease and pain avoidance gotten us? There are ample indications that many of us feel something is lacking or lost or inexplicable in our lives. We hear observers of our culture use words such as *alienated, unsettled,* and *restless* to describe many of us. Violence, depression, and anxiety are increasing. For example, Mary Pipher says,

> Many of us do work that we neither feel proud of nor enjoy. We are too rushed to do the things we really value...With more entertainment we are more bored. With more sexual

information and stimulation, we experience less sexual pleasure. In a culture focused on feelings, people grow emotionally numb. With more time-saving devices we have less time. With more books, we have fewer readers. With more mental health professionals, we have worse mental health...We wake in the night sorry for ourselves and our planet.[3]

Furthermore, where has contemporary church marketing gotten us? At the same time that many of us feel something is lacking in our lives, signs of a deep spiritual hunger are all around us. Note, for example, how full retreat centers are, or the books on spirituality that pop up on best-seller lists. And yet, in this climate of unease and of spiritual hunger, attendance in our churches is declining! Is it possible that our church marketing strategies that appeal to people's ego-centeredness and, consequently, the kind of interests people often bring to church with them has no appeal for many genuine spiritual seekers?

In such a moment, Mark's story itself may be a disturbing, disrupting event in our lives! It tells us that ego-centeredness and running away in fear will not lead us home to ourselves. It tells us that our religious practices and beliefs are no substitute for insightfulness and no indicator of where our allegiance ultimately lies. Whether we are inside the church or outside, Mark's story insists we only receive the *basileia* of God when we receive it like children, that is, like those not invested in furthering our self-centered interests. The Way of the Lord is difficult indeed, but we are promised spiritual help and guidance. And Mark shows that it is the way home. Thus, Mark may be preparing us for a summons from God to begin our spiritual journeys. Or to begin our spiritual journeys again. Or to take a turn on our journeys and go down a road we never thought we'd travel.

> "He is risen. He is going before you into Galilee. There you will see him, just as he told you."

There Mark leaves us, as he should. For only we can answer our summons.

So...anyone bound for Galilee?

Notes

Introduction

[1]"How All Stories Came Among Men," recounted in *African Myths and Tales,* ed. Susan Feldman (New York: Dell Publishing, 1963), 170–73.

[2]Quoted in Jack Kornfield and Christina Feldman, *Soul Food: Stories to Nourish the Spirit and the Heart* (San Francisco: Harper San Francisco, 1996).

[3]I count myself among the majority of biblical scholars who hold to the hypothesis that Mark was the first gospel written and became a source for Matthew and Luke. I believe this hypothesis makes the best sense of the evidence available to make such judgments.

[4]Quoted in Robin Deen Carnes and Sally Craig, *Sacred Circles: A Guide to Creating Your Own Women's Spirituality Group* (San Francisco: Harper San Francisco, 1998), 69.

[5]Herbert Anderson and Edward Foley, *Mighty Stories, Dangerous Rituals: Weaving Together the Human and the Divine* (San Francisco: Jossey-Bass, 1998), 4.

[6]John Shea, *An Experience Named Spirit* (Allen, Tex.: Thomas More, 1983), 107.

[7]I am indebted to Dr. Edward Thornton for these three classifications of stories (those that entertain, those that teach a moral, those that touch us spiritually) presented in a class on "The Psychology of the Religious Experience" at the Southern Baptist Theological Seminary, Louisville, Ky., fall 1984.

[8]These particular perspectives on stories are taken from Megan McKenna and Tony Cowan, *Keepers of the Story* (Maryknoll, N.Y.: Orbis Books, 1997); and William R. White, *Stories for Telling: A Treasury for Christian Storytellers* (Minneapolis: Augsburg Publishing House, 1986). White calls these kinds of stories "true stories."

[9]As a person of faith, my understanding of what it means to be human is theological. As my teacher and friend Molly Marshall has observed, "The human person cannot be fully explained or understood by any observable scientific method. In addition to these studies, our distinctiveness as human beings requires a theological interpretation." (*What It Means to be Human* [Macon, Ga.: Smith and Helwys, 1995], 24–25.) I am indebted to Dorothee Soelle, *Death by Bread Alone: Text and Reflections on Religious Experiences,* trans. David L. Scheidt (Philadelphia: Fortress Press, 1978) for the language used here to describe being authentically human.

[10]Sallie McFague, *Speaking in Parables* (Philadelphia: Fortress Press, 1975), 138.

[11]C. S. Song, *The Believing Heart: An Invitation to Story Theology* (Minneapolis: Fortress Press, 1999), 67.

[12]I am indebted to McKenna and Cowan, *Keepers of the Story;* Barry Lopez, *Crossing Open Ground* (New York: Vintage Books, 1989), 71; and Connie Regan-Blake of The Folktellers for the language used here to describe the stories of the divine-human encounter.

[13]From "Storytelling as the Language of Faith," found on http://www.tejasstorytelling.com/faith.html in July 2001.

[14]Dorothee Soelle, *Against the Wind: Memoir of a Radical Christian,* trans. Barbara and Martin Rumscheidt (Minneapolis: Fortress Press, 1999), 33.

[15]Shea, *An Experience Named Spirit,* 65.

[16]Soelle, *Against the Wind,* 31.

[17]Jane Yolen, "Introduction," in *Favorite Folktales from Around the World,* ed. Jane Yolen (New York: Pantheon Books, 1986), 7.

[18]This version of this much-told story is taken from John Shea, "Theology and Autobiography: Relating Theology to Lived Experience," *Commonweal* 105 (1978): 360.

[19]Dr. Seuss, *Horton Hears a Who* (New York: Random House, 1954), 32.

[20]A. A. Milne, "In Which Tigger Is Un-Bounced," in *The House at Pooh Corner* (New York: Dutton's Children's Books, 1928).

[21]Berkeley Breathed, *A Wish for Wings That Work* (Boston: Little, Brown and Co., 1991).

[22]See the similar perspective offered by Parker J. Palmer, *The Active Life: Wisdom for Work, Creativity, and Caring* (San Francisco: Harper San Francisco, 1991), 99. For those who are interested, here is a more detailed explanation of the method of reading I am using. Reading Mark alongside the stories will first allow us to glimpse where truths about being authentically human might lie within the gospel. That is, we will read with an eye toward noticing when a pattern or motif appears "all over the place"–in *good* stories and also in Mark.

We will view such a pattern or motif as a hint that some "humanly shared, virtually universal, basic existential concern about the human condition is being signaled to us " (Susan Niditch, *Folklore and the Hebrew Bible* [Minneapolis: Fortress Press, 1993], 23). Next we will examine these hints by means of the sociohistorical, narrative, and feminist critical methods of biblical scholars. Thus, we will know better whether the "underlying layer of inspired truth" that we suspect is in the text is actually there, or whether we are trying to make the text say what we want it to say. We will also know more of what Mark says about it. Finally, we will turn to other *good* stories yet again. Reading the stories after our exegesis helps us see with greater clarity what Mark can teach us about being authentically human.

²³Song, *The Believing Heart,* 66.

²⁴A third disclaimer that might be helpful to some readers is that I am drawing on the work of storytellers, folklorists, and cultural anthropologists rather than narrative theologians for my understanding of and work with stories. While both groups talk about stories, they are doing quite different things with them. I am more interested in stories as intrinsic to what it means to be human than as a theological category for understanding the cultural-linguistic character of communities of faith.

Chapter 1: The Beginning of the Story

¹Dante Alighieri, *Dante's Divine Comedy: Inferno, Journey to Joy,* trans. and retold by Kathryn Lindskoog (Macon, Ga.: Mercer University Press, 1997), 23–24, 32.

²See such sources for mystical teachings about the ascent to God as Michael Cox, *Handbook of Christian Spirituality: A Guide to Figures and Teachings from the Biblical Era to the Twentieth Century* (San Francisco: Harper and Row, 1983); Harvey D. Egan, *Christian Mysticism: The Future of a Tradition* (New York: Pueblo Publishing Co., 1984); *Christian Spirituality: The Essential Guide to the Most Influential Spiritual Writings of the Christian Tradition,* ed. Frank N. Magill and Ian P. McGreal (San Francisco: Harper and Row, 1988).

³See such sources for these perspectives on journey stories as Joseph Campbell, *The Hero with a Thousand Faces,* 2d ed. (Princeton: Princeton University Press, 1968), 40; Dorothee Soelle, *Death by Bread Alone: Texts and Reflections on Religious Experience,* trans. David L. Scheidt (Philadelphia: Fortress Press, 1978), 47; Phil Cousineau, *The Art of Pilgrimage: The Seeker's Guide to Making Travel Sacred* (Berkeley, Calif.: Conari Press, 1998). I am also greatly indebted to my teacher Dr. Edward E. Thornton for sharing his unpublished manuscript *To Hell and Beyond: Images of the Spiritual Journey in Dante's* Comedy (1987), with his students. I have drawn from this work as well.

⁴I love this language from Campbell, *Hero with a Thousand Faces,* 35.

⁵Soelle, *Death by Bread Alone,* 48.

⁶Scholars disagree on which of these events in the stories make up a new stage of the journey. Campbell, in *Hero with a Thousand Faces,* describes three stages: departure (including summons, supernatural aid, crossing the first threshold, the belly of the whale), initiation (including the road of trials and achieving the goal among other experiences), and the return; while Thornton, in our 1984 class, described four stages: departure (including summons and supernatural aid), crossing the first threshold, initiation (including road of trials and achieving the goal), and the return of the liberator. Rather than concern myself with which of these events make up separate stages or go together in a single stage of the journey, I am interested in all these events as nearly universal components of journey stories.

⁷Soelle, *Death by Bread Alone,* 51.

⁸Ibid., 128–29; Thornton, *To Hell and Beyond.*

⁹Joan Chittister, *Light in the Darkness: New Reflections on the Psalms for Every Day of the Year* (New York: Crossroad, 1998), 118.

¹⁰Quoted in Soelle, *Death by Bread Alone,* 61.

¹¹Thornton, *To Hell and Beyond,* iii.

¹²Werner H. Kelber, *Mark's Story of Jesus* (Philadelphia: Fortress Press, 1979), 17.

¹³David Rhoads and Donald Michie, *Mark as Story: An Introduction to the Narrative of a Gospel* (Philadelphia: Fortress Press, 1982), 64.

¹⁴Diarmuid McGann, in his book *The Journeying Self: The Gospel of Mark Through a Jungian Perspective* (New York: Paulist Press, 1985), read Mark by means of a journey theme. But he did so by imposing a Jungian perspective on the gospel and meditating on what he saw

through that lens rather than by exegeting and examining the journey contained within Mark's story. His work is fine as it is, but it is quite different from what I am proposing to do.

[15]Soelle, *Death by Bread Alone,* 47.

[16]I am indebted to Donald H. Juel, *A Master of Surprise: Mark Interpreted* (Minneapolis: Fortress Press, 1994), 35–36, for this insight.

[17]Cousineau, *Art of Pilgrimage,* 83.

[18]"The Golden Bird," in *The Complete Brothers Grimm Fairy Tales,* ed. Lily Owens (New York: Portland House, 1997), 210, 213.

[19]John Bunyan, *The Pilgrim's Progress* (1678; reprint, Old Tappan, N.J.: Fleming H. Revel Co., 1980), 18.

[20]See such sources on the wilderness and its impact on the spiritual life as Roberta C. Bondi, *To Pray and To Love: Conversations on Prayer with the Early Church* (Minneapolis: Fortress Press, 1991); Demetrius Dumm, *Flowers in the Desert: A Spirituality of the Bible* (New York: Paulist Press, 1987); Kenneth Leach, *Experiencing God: Theology as Spirituality* (San Francisco: Harper and Row, 1985).

[21]Ched Myers, Marie Dennis, Joseph Nangle, Cynthia Moe-Lobeda, Stuart Taylor, *"Say to This Mountain": Mark's Story of Discipleship* (Maryknoll, N.Y.: Orbis, 1996), 8.

[22]Here I have used the wonderful translation of these verses contained in *The Five Books of Moses: A New Translation with Introductions, Commentary, and Notes by Everett Fox* (New York: Schocken Books, Inc., 1995).

[23]Susan R. Garrett, *The Temptations of Jesus in Mark's Gospel* (Grand Rapids, Mich.: Wm. B. Eerdmans, 1998), 57.

[24]Soelle, *Death by Bread Alone,* 72.

[25]I am deeply indebted to Thornton, *To Hell and Beyond,* 64, for showing me the importance of Dante's inscription for whether or not we continue our journey.

[26]The Greek word *basileia* can mean kingdom (the usual choice in New Testament translations), kingly realm, domain, empire, monarchy, kingly rule, sovereignty, dominion, or reign. How to best translate? Choosing one of the above options eliminates the others and removes the ambiguity of the word. Further, most of these options ascribe imperial power to God, which is exactly how God does not exercise power, according to Mark. Therefore, I follow the lead of Elisabeth Schüssler Fiorenza and simply transliterate the word, thus allowing it to evoke its whole range of meanings. See Elisabeth Schüssler Fiorenza, *Jesus: Miriam's Child, Sophia's Prophet* (New York: Continuum, 1994), 92.

[27]See Bondi, *To Pray and to Love,* 101–3, for a more full and quite wonderful treatment of monastic teaching on the virtue of humility.

[28]J. R. R. Tolkien, *Lord of the Rings, Volume I: The Fellowship of the Ring* (Boston: Houghton Mifflin, 1965), 51.

[29]Bunyan, *Pilgrim's Progress,* 13–14.

[30]See the article on such seminary students by Lyric Wallwork Winik, "When *The Call* Comes Later in Life," *Parade Magazine,* Oct. 17, 1999. Interestingly, the cover of the magazine announces the article with this quote in large print: "There Must Be More To Life."

[31]Bunyan, *Pilgrim's Progress,* 59.

[32]Martin E. Marty, *A Cry of Absence* (San Francisco: Harper and Row, 1983), 5–6.

[33]Quoted in Bondi, *To Pray and to Love,* 43.

[34]I am borrowing the language of Saint John of the Cross, *Dark Night of the Soul,* trans. and ed. E. Allison Peers (Garden City, N.Y.: Image Books, 1959), 36, 91, 100, which are among the pages where this language is used.

Chapter 2:"See What You Hear!"

[1]I am drawing on Nina Jaffe's retelling of "The Strange Journey of Rabbi Joshua ben Levi," in her book *The Mysterious Visitor: Stories of the Prophet Elijah* (New York: Scholastic Press, 1997); the quote is from page 82.

[2]Edward E. Thornton, *To Hell and Beyond: Images of the Spiritual Journey in Dante's* Comedy (unpublished manuscript, 1987), 102.

[3]Wilhelm Michaelis, "orao," in *Theological Dictionary of the New Testament,* vol. 5, ed. Gerhard Friedrich and Geoffrey W. Bromily, trans. Geoffrey W. Bromily (Grand Rapids: Wm. B. Eerdmans, 1967), 343–44.

[4]For further details on Jesus' liberating people from whatever binds them, see my comments in Mitzi Minor, *The Spirituality of Mark: Responding to God* (Louisville: Westminster John Knox Press, 1996), 57.

[5]The language here is Donald H. Juel's, from *A Master of Surprise: Mark Interpreted* (Minneapolis: Fortress Press, 1994), 86.

[6]The other two imperatives to see in chapter 13 will be addressed later.

[7]The Greek word in 15:39 is not *blepo* but the aorist participle *idon*, which is technically a form of another Greek word that means "see," *orao*. But Mark only uses the aorist form of *orao* for his "past" tense for *see*. Indeed, in all of the New Testament the aorist form of *blepo* is used only once, in Revelation 22:8. Consequently, it seems reasonable to understand this use of *idon* as the kind of sight we've been discovering in Mark's use of *blepo*.

[8]I am borrowing language from Phil Cousineau, *The Art of Pilgrimage: The Seeker's Guide to Making Travel Sacred* (Berkeley, Calif.: Conari Press, 1998), 99–100.

[9]As told in Anthony de Mello, *Taking Flight: A Book of Story Meditations* (New York: Image Books, 1990), 53.

[10]John Shea, *Elijah at the Wedding Feast and Other Tales: Stories of the Human Spirit* (Chicago: ACTA Publications, 1999), 27–28.

[11]A growing number of scholars are reading the widow's story this way. See Minor, *The Spirituality of Mark,* 87; Ched Myers, *Binding the Strong Man: A Political Reading of Mark's Story of Jesus* (Maryknoll, N.Y.: Orbis Books, 1988), 320–21; A. Wright, "The Widow's Mite: Praise or Lament? A Matter of Context," *Catholic Biblical Quarterly* 44 (1982): 262.

[12]See Myers, *Binding the Strong Man,* 320–21, for details of ways scholars believe scribes were able to "devour" widows' houses in first-century Palestine.

[13]For details of the redistribution economy centered in the temple, see John H. Elliot, "Temple Versus Household in Luke-Acts: A Contrast in Social Institutions," in *The Social World of Luke-Acts: Models for Interpretation,* ed. Jerome H. Neyrey (Peabody, Mass.: Hendrickson Publishers, 1991), 233–35; Myers, *Binding the Strong Man,* 300–301.

[14]John Shea, *The Legend of the Bells and Other Tales: Stories of the Human Spirit* (Chicago: ACTA Publications, 1996), 111–12.

[15]I am drawing from the version of this story translated and retold by Anthea Bell and published in the United States by North-South Books, 1986.

[16]I have borrowed language from Cousineau, *Art of Pilgrimage,* 121.

[17]Mary Pipher, *Reviving Ophelia: Saving the Selves of Adolescent Girls* (New York: Ballantine Books, 1995), 23.

[18]The phrase "United States of Advertising" is from Mary Pipher, *The Shelter of Each Other: Rebuilding Our Families* (New York: Ballantine Books, 1997), 32.

[19]Clinton McCann, "If It Makes You Happy," Todd Lectures given at Memphis Theological Seminary, Memphis, March, 1998. The quote about "getting all you can," however, is taken from a sermon I once heard David Garland preach years ago.

[20]Pipher, *Reviving Ophelia,* 183–85.

[21]Ched Myers, "God Speed the Year Jubilee: The Biblical Vision of Sabbath Economics," *Sojourners* (1998), 24–26.

[22]Research by Ryan and Kasser reported in Alfie Kohn, "Search for wealth, fame may also bring anxiety," The New York Times News Service, *The Commercial Appeal,* Memphis, Tenn., 7 February 1999.

[23]Quoted in Walker Percy, *Lost in the Cosmos: The Last Self-Help Book* (New York: Farrar, Straus, & Giroux, 1983), 179.

[24]Dorothee Soelle with Shirley A. Cloyes, *To Work and To Love* (Philadelphia: Fortress Press, 1984), 49, 62.

[25]Pipher, *The Shelter of Each Other,* 81.

[26]I am indebted to Daniel Berrigan, *Uncommon Prayer: A Book of Psalms* (Maryknoll, N.Y.: Orbis Books, 1978), 13, for this insight.

[27]Parker J. Palmer, *The Active Life: Wisdom for Work, Creativity, and Caring* (San Francisco: Harper San Francisco, 1991), 25.

[28]Richard Rohr, *Everything Belongs: The Gift of Contemplative Prayer* (New York: Crossroad Books, 1999), 28, 29.

[29]Dante Alighieri, *Dante's Divine Comedy: Purgatory, Journey to Joy, Part Two,* trans. and retold with notes by Kathryn Lindskoog (Macon, Ga.: Mercer University Press, 1997), 149, emphasis mine.

Chapter 3: "What Do You Wish That I Would Do for You?"

[1]This story is told in Parker J. Palmer, *The Active Life: Wisdom for Work, Creativity, and Caring* (San Francisco: Harper San Francisco, 1990), 27–28.

[2]The earliest treatment of this theme may have been in Joseph B. Tyson, "The Blindness of the Disciples in Mark," *Journal of Biblical Literature* 80 (1961): 261–68.

[3]Paul J. Achtemeier, "Mark 9:30–37," *Interpretation* 30 (1976),182; Bruce J. Malina and Richard Rohrbaugh, *Social Science Commentary on the Synoptic Gospels* (Minneapolis: Augsburg Fortress, 1992), 238, note that children had little status in the families of that time: "A child was on a par with a slave, and only after reaching maturity was he/she a free person who could inherit the family estate. The term child/children could also be used as a serious insult (see Mt. 11:16–17)."

[4]How to make "Son of Man" inclusive continues to be a thorny issue for me. I believe "New Human Being" is what Mark intended with the term, but until we get more familiar with this or another new, more inclusive way of understanding "Son of man," I choose to "slash it" in order for readers to know that "New Human Being" refers to the old "Son of man."

[5]David Rhoads and Donald Michie, *Mark as Story: An Introduction to the Narrative of a Gospel* (Philadelphia: Fortress Press, 1982), 101.

[6]See Rhoads and Michie, *Mark as Story*, 130–34; and Jack Dean Kingsbury, *Conflict in Mark: Jesus, Authorities, Disciples* (Minneapolis: Fortress Press, 1989), 24–27, for discussion of these traits of the minor characters and their use as foils in the gospel. I should note that not all the minor characters exhibit both these traits, but that these traits are common to this character group.

[7]See Mitzi Minor, *The Spirituality of Mark: Responding to God* (Louisville: Westminster John Knox Press, 1996), 47–52, for a full treatment of this surprising story.

[8]See, e.g., Kingsbury, *Conflict in Mark*, 80–84; Rhoads and Michie, *Mark as Story*, 118.

[9]Sharon H. Ringe, "Solidarity and Contextuality: Readings of Matthew 18:21–35," in *Reading from This Place*, vol. 1, ed. Fernando F. Segovia and Mary Ann Tolbert (Minneapolis: Fortress, 1995), 199–212.

[10]Elisabeth Schüssler Fiorenza, *Jesus: Miriam's Child, Sophia's Prophet* (New York: Continuum, 1994), 12–18.

[11]Among many sources that can help us understand the "place" of the characters in Mark's story are Malina and Rohrbaugh, *Social Science Commentary on the Synoptic Gospels*.

[12]We should note that New Testament scholars using the social sciences in their study believe that first-century Mediterranean people had a different sense of self than we do today. These folk had collectivist or dyadic selves, which requires an in-group to know who one is (in contrast to contemporary Americans' individualistic selves). Even so, persons in collectivist societies can still be self-centered, but in that context the term would mean they have an "overly bloated and exaggerated" focus on their in-group. See, for example, Bruce J. Malina, "'Let Him Deny Himself' (Mark 8:34 & Par): A Social Psychological Model of Self-Denial," *Biblical Theology Bulletin* 24(1994), 106–19.

[13]Kingsbury, *Conflict in Mark*, 78, interprets the charge in 14:57–58 thusly.

[14]See Minor, *Spirituality of Mark*, 91–92, for this interpretation of 11:20–25.

[15]I am using the version of this story found in Henri J. M. Nouwen, *The Wounded Healer* (Garden City, N.Y.: Image Books, 1979), 81–82.

[16]I am drawing on the version of this story that appears in Megan McKenna and Tony Cowan, *Keepers of the Story* (Maryknoll, N. Y.: Orbis Books, 1997), 121.

[17]I have shortened the version of this story that appears in McKenna and Cowan, *Keepers of the Story*, 124–25.

[18]Versions of this story can be found in many places, including William R. White, *Stories for Telling: A Treasury for Christian Storytellers* (Minneapolis: Augsburg, 1986), 48–51; Edward E. Thornton, *Being Transformed: An Inner Way of Spiritual Growth* (Philadelphia: Westminster Press, 1984), 92.

[19]I am drawing on the version of this story found in Nouwen, *Wounded Healer*, 25–26.

[20]Nathaniel Hawthorne, *The Scarlet Letter* (1850; reprint, New York: Washington Square Press, 1994), 67.

[21]As told in Robert A. Johnson, *Owning Your Own Shadow: Understanding the Dark Side of the Psyche* (San Francisco: Harper San Francisco, 1991), vii–viii.

[22]Fyodor Dostoevsky, "The Grand Inquisitor," in *The Brothers Karamazov*, trans. Andrew H. MacAndrew (1880; reprint, New York: Bantam Books, 1970), 306–9.

[23]My friend and colleague at Memphis Theological Seminary, Paul Dekar, whose area is Missions and Evangelism, recommends Brian Stanley, *The Bible and The Flag* (Leicaster, England: Apollos, 1990) as a balanced treatment of the issue of missions and imperialism.

[24]Karen Kijewski, *Alley Kat Blues* (New York: Doubleday, 1995), 69.

[25]McKenna and Cowan, *Keepers of the Story*, 199.

Chapter 4: "Do Not Be Afraid, Only Believe"

[1]Dante Alighieri, *Dante's Divine Comedy: Purgatory, The Journey to Joy, Part 2,* trans. and retold with notes by Kathryn Lindskoog (Macon, Ga.: Mercer University Press, 1997), 153–54.

[2]Parker J. Palmer, *The Courage to Teach: Exploring the Inner Landscape of a Teacher's Life* (San Francisco: Jossey-Bass Publishers, 1998), 39. Gavin de Becker, in *The Gift of Fear: Survival Signals That Protect Us from Violence* (Boston: Little, Brown, and Co., 1997), would argue that the examples given here, and indeed much of what we call fear, should more precisely be called worry or anxiety. I suspect he is correct. Since the stories, Mark, and we ourselves most often speak of *fear,* however, I will do so as well.

[3]Edward E. Thornton, *Being Transformed: An Inner Way of Spiritual Growth* (Philadelphia: Westminster Press, 1984), 102.

[4]Ibid., 103–4.

[5]Palmer, *Courage to Teach,* 38.

[6]Fyodor Dostoevsky, "The Grand Inquisitor" in *The Brothers Karamazov*, trans. Andrew H. MacAndrew (1880; reprint, New York: Bantam Books, 1970), 316.

[7]Ibid., 304–5, emphasis mine.

[8]Ibid, 301, 310, emphasis mine.

[9]Ibid., 308.

[10]Ibid., 312, emphasis mine.

[11]Ibid., 313.

[12]Ibid., 316.

[13]Kenneth Grahame, *The Wind in the Willows* (1908; reprint, New York: Charles Scribner's Sons, 1961), 134–35.

[14]Ibid., 136.

[15]Rudolf Otto, *The Idea of the Holy,* 2d ed., trans. John W. Harvey (London: Oxford University Press, 1950), 31.

[16]Palmer, *Courage to Teach,* 37.

[17]Kathleen Norris, *Amazing Grace: A Vocabulary of Faith* (New York: Riverhead Books, 1998), 146.

[18]See Mitzi Minor, *The Spirituality of Mark: Responding to God* (Louisville: Westminster John Knox Press, 1996), 42–43, for a more full treatment of God alone controlling the sea.

[19]Mary Oliver, "Maybe," in *House of Light* (Boston: Beacon Press, 1990), 77; emphasis mine.

[20]Norris, *Amazing Grace,* 144.

[21]Palmer, *Courage to Teach,* 38.

[22]Ibid., 57.

[23]John Shea, *The Legend of the Bells and Other Tales: Stories of the Human Spirit* (Chicago: ACTA Publications, 1996), 74.

[24]Norris, *Amazing Grace,* 144–45.

[25]Dante, *Purgatory,* 154; emphasis mine.

[26]"Jumping Mouse" in Shea, *The Legend of the Bells,* 63–72.

[27]Ibid., 75.

[28]Charles Dickens, *A Christmas Carol* (1843; reprint, New York: Washington Square Press, 1967), 43.

[29]Ibid., 162.

[30]Ibid., 217–18.

[31]Richard Rohr, *Everything Belongs: The Gift of Contemplative Prayer* (New York: Crossroad Books, 1996), 55. `

[32]J. Clinton McCann, "If It Makes You Happy…Psalms 1–2," Todd Lectures, given at Memphis Theological Seminary, Memphis, Tenn., March 1998.

[33]Mary Pipher, *The Shelter of Each Other: Rebuilding Our Families* (New York: Ballantine Books, 1996), 15, 26.

[34]Rohr, *Everything Belongs,* 55, 68.

[35]Dorothee Soelle, *Death by Bread Alone: Texts and Reflections on Religious Experience,* trans. David L. Scheidt (Philadelphia: Fortress Press, 1978), 69.

[36]Roberta Bondi, *To Love as God Loves: Conversations with the Early Church* (Philadelphia: Fortress Press, 1987), 29, 42–43.

[37]As told in Martin Buber, *Tales of the Hasidim: The Later Masters* (New York: Schocken Books, 1947), 249–50.

[38]Rohr, *Everything Belongs,* 66; I am also indebted to Bondi, *To Love as God Loves,* 47; and Thornton, *Being Transformed,* 72, for the information and language of this paragraph.

Chapter 5: The End of the Story

[1]J. R.R. Tolkien, *The Two Towers, Being the 2nd Part of the Lord of the Rings,* 2d ed. (Boston: Houghton, Mifflin Co., 1965), 97–98.

[2]Frank Kermode, *The Genesis of Secrecy: On the Interpretation of Narrative* (Cambridge: Harvard University Press, 1979), 53–73. There are many studies of endings of stories, including studies of the ending of Mark's story. I have relied, in addition to Kermode, on the following biblical scholars: R. Alan Culpepper, *Anatomy of the Fourth Gospel* (Philadelphia: Fortress Press, 1994); Beverly R. Gaventa, "John 21 and the Problem of Narrative Closure," in *Exploring the Gospel of John,* ed. R. Alan Culpepper and C. Clifton Black (Louisville: Westminster John Knox Press, 1996), 240–52; Norman R. Petersen, "When Is the End Not the End? Literary Reflections on the Ending of Mark's Narrative," *Interpretation* 34 (1980), 151–66.

[3]For readers who may not be aware, the oldest and best manuscripts of Mark end at 16:8. The endings that appear in many Bibles today were not part of the original gospel of Mark. I believe, along with what seems to be the majority of Markan scholars, that the weight of evidence suggests that Mark intended to end his story at 16:8.

[4]The so-called "shorter ending" of Mark, which adds approximately two sentences to v. 8, is usually dated from the fourth century. The longer ending of Mark, which is verses 9–20 in many Bibles, appears to have been added to the gospel in the late second century.

[5]Petersen, "When is the End Not the End?" 153.

[6]Thomas E. Boomershine, "Mark 16:8 and the Apostolic Commission," *Journal of Biblical Literature* 100 (1981), 237.

[7]R. Alan Culpepper, "The Passion and Resurrection in Mark," *Review and Expositor* 75 (1978), 597. Other scholars who interpret Mark's ending similarly include Brian K. Blount, *Go Preach! Mark's Kingdom Message and the Black Church Today* (Maryknoll, N.Y.: Orbis, 1998), 189; Mary Ann Tolbert, *Sowing the Gospel: Mark's World in Literary-Historical Perspective* (Minneapolis: Fortress Press, 1989), 297–99.

[8]The Greek word used here is not *blepo* but the future tense *opsomai,* which is the future form of another Greek word for *see,* which was no longer being used in present tense. Mark, however, only uses *opsomai* as his future form for *see.* Consequently, we may look to "see" if Mark also may mean something other than literal sight in this verse.

[9]Petersen, "When is the End Not the End?" 163.

[10]Ibid. Other scholars who believe Mark pointed toward a meeting between the risen Jesus and disciples in Galilee, though their readings are not the same as Petersen's, include Hugh Anderson, *The Gospel of Mark,* The New Century Bible Commentary (Grand Rapids: Wm. B. Eerdmans, 1976), 357; Reginald H. Fuller, *The Formation of the Resurrection Narratives* (Philadelphia: Fortress Press, 1971), 64–67; Vincent Taylor, *The Gospel According to St. Mark,* 2d ed., Thornapple Commentaries (1966; reprint, Grand Rapids: Baker Book House, 1981), 608.

[11]Included among these scholars are Ernst Lohmeyer, *Galilaa und Jerusalem* (Gottingen, 1936); Willi Marxsen, *Mark the Evangelist: Studies on the Redaction History of the Gospel* (Nashville: Abingdon, 1969), 75ff, 111ff; Norman Perrin, *The Resurrection According to Matthew, Mark and Luke* (Philadelphia: Fortress Press, 1977), 27, 31.

[12]Among a number of scholars who treat Galilee as place and symbol in Mark, see Elizabeth Struthers Malbon, *Narrative Space and Mythic Meaning in Mark* (San Francisco: Harper & Row, 1986), 25–46.

[13]Joseph Campbell, *The Hero with a Thousand Faces,* 2d ed. (Princeton: Princeton University Press, 1968), 193, 217.

[14]Edward R. Thornton, *To Hell and Beyond: Images of the Spiritual Journey in Dante's* Comedy, unpublished manuscript, 1987, 1.

[15]Clarissa Pinkola Estes, *Women Who Run with the Wolves: Myths and Stories of the Wild Woman Archetype* (New York: Ballantine Books, 1992), 77–82.

[16]J. R. R. Tolkien, *The Hobbit* (Ballantine Books, 1973), 299–300.

[17]T. S. Eliot, *Four Quartets* (New York: Harcourt Brace and Company, 1943), 59.

[18]Dorothee Soelle, *Death by Bread Alone: Texts and Reflections on Religious Experience*, trans. David L. Scheidt (Philadelphia: Fortress Press, 1978), 68–69, 126, 135.

[19]Howard Clark Kee, *Community of the New Age: Studies in Mark's Gospel* (1977; reprint, Macon, Ga.: Mercer University Press, 1983), 100.

[20]Blount, *Go Preach!* 9–10.

[21]See Ched Myers, *Binding the Strong Man: A Political Reading of Mark's Story of Jesus* (Maryknoll, N.Y.: Orbis, 1988), 246, for this understanding of "take up your cross."

[22]For those interested, here are exegetical details about the other two places apocalyptic hope and resurrection are linked. After the transfiguration experience, Jesus ordered the disciples not to relate the vision until he had risen from the dead (9:9). The disciples, questioning among themselves the meaning of rising from the dead (9:10), ask Jesus, "Why do the scribes say that Elijah must come first?" (9:11), that is, first before the rising from the dead. Their question comes from the belief, from Malachi 4:5–6 and held in some Jewish circles, that Elijah would be the forerunner of the age to come. Thus, the conversations here associate resurrection with the age to come. In the last reference, the Sadducees ask Jesus about levirate marriage "in *the* resurrection" (12:23). Their question raises the issue of the general resurrection that takes place at the end of the present age and the start of the age to come. In his response Jesus ridicules their lack of knowledge of both the scriptures and God while affirming resurrection (12:25–27). For our purposes again, we should not miss the association of resurrection with the apocalyptic hope for the new age to come.

[23]N. T. Wright, *The New Testament and the People of God* (Minneapolis: Fortress Press, 1992), 299–334. Brian Blount, *Go Preach!* 67–70, concurs with Wright.

[24]Blount, *Go Preach!* 71–72.

[25]Wright, *The New Testament and the People of God,* 328.

[26]See Thorwald Lorenzen, *Resurrection and Discipleship: Interpretive Models, Biblical Reflections, Theological Consequences* (Maryknoll, N.Y.: Orbis, 1995), 146.

[27]Parker J. Palmer, *The Active Life: Wisdom for Work, Creativity, and Caring* (San Francisco: Harper San Francisco, 1990), 141–42.

[28]Ibid.

[29]Julia Esquivel, "They Have Threatened Us with Resurrection," in *Threatened with Resurrection*, 2d ed. (Elgin, Ill.: Brethren Press, 1994), 59, 61. The St. Pauli is apparently a bar.

[30]J. R. R. Tolkien, *The Return of the King: The Lord of the Rings, Part Three* (1955; reprint, New York: Ballantine Books, 1965), 234.

[31]Frances Hodgson Burnett, *The Secret Garden* (1911; reprint, New York: Dover Publications, 1994), 45, 57, 70–71.

[32]As told in John Shea, *The Legend of the Bells and Other Tales* (Chicago: ACTA Publications, 1996), 64–65.

[33]Burnett, *Secret Garden,* 76.

Conclusion

[1]Dr. Farley's lecture has been published as "Are There Types of Faith? Radical Faith and Narcissistic Religion," *Memphis Theological Seminary Journal* 36 (1998): 27–37.

[2]Dorothee Soelle, *The Strength of the Weak: Toward a Christian Feminist Identity,* trans. Robert and Rita Kimber (Philadelphia: Westminster Press, 1984), 24–30.

[3]Mary Pipher, *The Shelter of Each Other: Rebuilding Our Families* (New York: Ballantine Books, 1996), 81.